Prayers for All Seasons

Based on the
Revised Common Lectionary
Year B

Prayers for All Seasons

Based on the
Revised Common Lectionary

Year B

Seasons
OF THE Spirit™
COLLECTION

Editor: Ellen Turnbull
Cover design: Cyrus Gandevia
Interior and pre-press production: Cyrus Gandevia
Cover image: © R.J. Seymour/iStockphoto
Proofreader: Dianne Greenslade

WoodLake is an imprint of Wood Lake Publishing, Inc. Wood Lake Publishing acknowledges the financial support of the Government of Canada, through the Canada Book Fund for its publishing activities. Wood Lake Publishing also acknowledges the financial support of the Province of British Columbia through the Book Publishing Tax Credit.

At Wood Lake Publishing, we practise what we publish, being guided by a concern for fairness, justice, and equal opportunity in all of our relationships with employees and customers. Wood Lake Publishing is committed to caring for the environment and all creation. Wood Lake Publishing recycles, reuses, and encourages readers to do the same. Resources are printed on 30% post-consumer recycled paper and more environmentally friendly groundwood papers (newsprint), whenever possible. A percentage of all profit is donated to charitable organizations.

Library and Archives Canada Cataloguing in Publication

Prayers for all seasons : based on the Revised common lectionary year B / compiled by Ellen Turnbull.

Includes index.
ISBN 978-1-77064-681-0 (pbk.)

1. Prayers. 2. Lectionaries. I. Turnbull, Ellen, compiler II. Title: Common lectionary (1992). Year B

BV264.13.P73 2014   264'.13   C2014-900644-6

Copyright © Wood Lake Publishing Inc.
Use of these prayers in congregations for worship is encouraged; they may be reproduced for this purpose without permission. All rights reserved. With the sole exception noted above, no part of this publication may be reproduced – except in the case of brief quotations embodied in critical articles and reviews – stored in an electronic retrieval system, or transmitted in any form or by any means, electronic, mechanical, photocopying, recording, or otherwise, without prior written permission of the publisher or copyright holder.

Published by Woodlake
An imprint of Wood Lake Publishing Inc.
485 Beaver Lake Road, Kelowna, BC, Canada, V4V 1S5
www.woodlakebooks.com
1.800.663.2775

Printing 10 9 8 7 6 5 4 3 2 1
Printed in Canada

CONTENTS

Season of Advent 7

Season of Christmas 17

Season after the Epiphany 23

Season of Lent 47

      Palm/ Passion Sunday 63

Season of Easter 67

      Pentecost Sunday 87

Season after Pentecost 91

Hebrew Scriptures Index 183

New Testament Index 185

SEASON OF ADVENT

Advent 1

(Year B begins on the first Sunday of Advent in 2014, 2017, 2020…)

LECTIONARY READINGS
Isaiah 64:1–9
Psalm 80:1–7, 17–19
1 Corinthians 1:3–9
Mark 13:24–37

Prayer after lighting the Advent candle (can be used each week during Advent).
Ask people to repeat each line.

God,
you gave us Jesus
and the story of Jesus is for the whole world.
May we light this candle
and may the flame remind us of Jesus
who brings hope to everyone.
Amen.

* * *

The following prayer is a contemporary Celtic caim – an encircling prayer which Celts used to affirm God's presence and protection. This also may be used each week during Advent as a call to worship.

Keep shadows without and light within;
    let your face shine that we may be saved.
Keep fear without and justice within;
    comfort, comfort your people.
Keep chaos without and life within;
    may those who sow in tears reap with shouts of joy.

Keep despair without and hope within;
>   deliver us that we may rejoice.
Come, O Advent God,
>   and reveal your promise in us now.

Our cry is one of longing, O God,
>   for a restored relationship with you.
As we enter the Season of Advent,
>   the longing is at its greatest.
It can be hard to find you in our world,
>   yet we believe you are here with us, renewing all
>   that is broken.
Come among us and, in flesh, abide with us,
>   that we may witness your presence around us,
>   and be filled with a new vision for your world.

* * *

One: We come a scattered people, tossed about like leaves in a storm.
Two: From the four winds,
All: gather us in, O God.
One: We come a worried people, minds filled with headlines of disaster.
Two: From the ends of the earth,
All: gather us in, O God.
One: We come a waiting people, yearning to see the face of God.
Two: From the ends of the heavens,
All: gather us in, O God.
One: Joining all the cosmos, the angels of heaven, and the peoples of earth, we come to worship our God.
Two: Gather us in your faithfulness and call us your people once more.
All: Gather us in, O God.

* * *

God, oil the hinges of our hearts' doors that they may swing gently and easily to welcome your coming. Amen. *(Prayer from Papua New Guinea)*

Advent 2

LECTIONARY READINGS
Isaiah 40:1–11
Psalm 85:1–2, 8–13
2 Peter 3:8–15a
Mark 1:1–8

Prayer after lighting the Advent candle (can be used each week during Advent). Ask people to repeat each line.

God,
you gave us Jesus
and the story of Jesus is for the whole world.
May we light this candle
and may the flame remind us of Jesus
who brings hope to everyone.
Amen.

* * *

God, our comfort and our strength, open our senses to hear your promise of liberation. Guide us to bring words and deeds of comfort and hope to the world. Amen.

* * *

Comfort us, O God,
    with a comfort that strengthens us for the world.
Comfort us, O God,
    with a comfort that encourages us to trust you.
Comfort us, O God,
    with a comfort that inspires us to be messengers of hope
    that our world may be transformed,
    and that it may begin here,
    in this place and among these people.
Comfort us, O God,
    with a comfort that renews our living and our worship.

* * *

One:	In the wild beauty of the wilderness
Two:	in the rush hour wildness of the city streets
All:	**we are called to prepare your way.**
One:	In the heavy heat of beach-waiting afternoons,
Two:	in the fierce cold of snow-driven mornings,
All:	**we are called to prepare your way.**
One:	When our way seems clear and the steps even,
Two:	when our path is winding and each step an effort,
All:	**we are called to prepare your way.**
One:	When all crowd around to hear your prophets,
Two:	when no one notices that you walk among us,
All:	**we are called to prepare your way.**

* * *

Sometimes we don't want to hear your words of forgiveness, Merciful One.
Sometimes we have done things that we don't think deserve to be forgiven.
There are people we have harmed who will never really forget
and there are people who have hurt us that we don't want to forgive.
How long will we hold ourselves and others unforgiven?
(silent pause)
Open our ears to your words of comfort.
Open our hearts to the mercy of your love.
Open our lives that we may once again be free.

* * *

May you know God's peace in words and ways of comfort.
May you show God's peace in words and ways of comfort.
May God's peace and hope shine in all the world.
Amen.

Advent 3

LECTIONARY READINGS
Isaiah 61:1–4, 8–11
Psalm 126 **or** Luke 1:47–55
1 Thessalonians 5:16–24
John 1:6–8, 19–28

Prayer after lighting the Advent candle (can be used each week during Advent).
Ask people to repeat each line.

God,
you gave us Jesus
and the story of Jesus is for the whole world.
May we light this candle
and may the flame remind us of Jesus
who brings hope to everyone.
Amen.

* * *

God of true joy, make us daring! Heal our broken hearts, free us from our prisons, and teach us to rejoice in your love through our acts of faithful living. Amen.

* * *

Spirit of the living God,
speak your word to us in this time of worship.
Fill us with true joy –
the joy that comes from knowing you;
the joy that comes
from feeling your justice come to life in our midst;
the joy that comes
as we truly prepare our hearts
as a dwelling place for the Messiah. Amen.

* * *

One: Take our guilt,
Two: and replace it with transcendent love *(pause)*.

One: Take our sorrow,
Two: and water our lives with compassion *(pause)*.

One: Take our selfishness,
Two: and reform it with a love for justice *(pause)*.

One: Take our barrenness,
Two: and impregnate us with hope *(pause)*.

One: Take our conflict,
Two: and infuse it with peace *(pause)*.

One: Take our world,
Two: and cram it with joy *(pause)*.

* * *

God is close,
and we will rejoice.
The world awaits,
and we will rejoice.
Incarnation is soon,
and we will rejoice.
God is restoring our fortunes,
and we will rejoice.
We shout with joy,
and we will rejoice.

Advent 4

LECTIONARY READINGS
2 Samuel 7:1–11, 16
Luke 1:47–55 **or** Psalm 89:1–4, 19–26
Romans 16:25–27
Luke 1:26–38

Prayer after lighting the Advent candle (can be used each week during Advent).
Ask people to repeat each line.

God,
you gave us Jesus
and the story of Jesus is for the whole world.
May we light this candle
and may the flame remind us of Jesus
who brings hope to everyone.
Amen.

* * *

Invite people during the response to hold their hands together as in prayer, and slowly open them and turn their palms upward.

One:	Sometimes we have ideas of how things should be, and we do not want to know of other options.
Two:	God of wonders,
All:	**help us to reveal your promise in our world.**
One:	Sometimes we think that God can only be found in certain places, or in certain ways.
Two:	God of no limits,
All:	**help us to reveal your promise in our world.**
One:	Sometimes we cannot believe the things that are asked of us, and assume we must be misunderstanding.
Two:	God of surprises,
All:	**help us to reveal your promise in our world.**

One: Sometimes we hear God calling us, and we let go of all of those things that hold us back and, like Mary, we say "nothing is impossible with God."
Two: God of wonders,
All: **help us to reveal your promise in our world. Amen.**

* * *

There are times, Comforting One, when I feel puzzled by what I sense your Spirit is leading me to do. In those times, I feel afraid and very alone. Let me hear, in my heart, the message to "not be afraid" and the reminder that you are with me. Amen.

* * *

Midwife God,
you promise to be with us, standing by our side when the pain comes and the labour of life seems unbearable.
We pray for those who suffer because of illness, poverty, injustice, and by whatever else their suffering is caused. *(Moment of silence or offer concerns aloud.)*
Come to us, O God,
and may we give birth to your promises.

Gentle mother of us all,
you create us, you enfold us, you hold us in your arms of care.
May we see your strong hand extend into the world to lift up the lowly and forgotten and bring justice and peace to all who wait. *(Moment of silence or offer concerns aloud.)*
Come to us, O God,
and may we give birth to your promises.

Incarnated One,
you pierced the shadows of our world with the light of heaven and became to us love in the flesh.
May we embrace you and hold you close to our lives so your presence can transform us into children of God. *(Moment of silence.)*
Come to us, O God,
and may we give birth to your promises.

* * *

One: May you be strengthened by the good news that God proclaimed in Jesus Christ.
May you be drawn to the wonder of the mystery revealed,
God's eternal love for us made flesh in Jesus Christ.
Go in the glory of God's abundant love.

**All: We go with hope
We go in peace.
We go with joy.
We go in love.
Thanks be to God.**

SEASON OF CHRISTMAS

Christmas Day

Proper 3 (A, B, C)

LECTIONARY READINGS
Isaiah 52:7–10
Psalm 98
Hebrews 1:1–4, (5–12)
John 1:1–14

Angel:	Do not be afraid! I bring you good news.
All:	**We who are poor and poor in spirit.**
Angel:	Take heart, Jesus Christ is born today.
All:	**We who falter under worldly rulers.**
Angel:	Take heart, the prince of peace has come.
All:	**We who yearn to be close to God.**
Angel:	Take heart, Jesus is Emmanuel, God with us. Do not be afraid, this good news is for all the earth. Lift up your hearts and sing with joy! Jesus Christ is born!

* * *

The skies of misty days are parted
with the radiant shining of never-ending love.
The Word breaks through into human life
and fills our empty silences with hope.
Thanks be to God! The Christ child is born.

The waiting earth is touched
with the footprints of new birth.
It lies there for us all to discover,
in its frailty and hope.
Thanks be to God! The Christ child is born.

The people look up in awe and wonder
and then we look downwards
and see the life of God among us here.
Thanks be to God! The Christ child is born.

* * *

On this day of days, loving God,
we gather to celebrate the wondrous gift of Jesus Christ,
born long ago
and still today,
child of the universe
present among us.
May we, in the things we do and say,
continue to give birth
to the presence of the living Christ
in our world today and always. Amen.

* * *

Christmas Caim
The following prayer is a contemporary Celtic caim – an encircling prayer which Celts used to affirm God's presence and protection. The worship leader journeys around the space encircling it, holding a lit candle and speaking the words below. The encircling finishes as the Christ candle is placed in the Advent wreath. Invite the congregation to face the leader as he or she moves around the space.

The life of the infant Christ
encircles us with surprising gifts:
Look outwards and see
an everlasting hope for good.
Look inward and find
each new possibility.
The life of the infant Christ
encircles us with surprising gifts:

Look beyond you and see
the light of the star
which beckons us on.
Look beside you and welcome
the company of love.
The life of the infant Christ
encircles us with surprising gifts:
Look widely and find
the Christ is near in friend and stranger.
Look closely and touch
the life of the divine within your own heart.
Stay, stay here now,
in the beauty of encircling love.

* * *

A child prays:
O Jesus Christ, we pray today for all children,
especially those whose lives are not happy.
We think of the ones who are not looking forward
to a lovely Christmas meal now
and who did not receive any presents this morning.
We pray for all children on this Christmas Day.

A mother prays:
O God, we pray for all mothers this day
who are anxious for their families.
We remember those who have little care around them
when they give birth
and who know that they will not be able
to feed their children well
or give them the comfort of a safe home.
We pray for those mothers who live in places of war,
or among other forms of violence,
and who long each day for peace and safety.
We pray for all mothers on this Christmas Day.

A father prays:
O God, we pray today for all fathers around the world.
We think especially of those
who tread life's journeys of fear with their families –
those who are refugees or desperately seeking work,
those who look out at empty fields
due to drought or floods
or who dread the next days
because they can see no future.
We pray for all fathers on this Christmas Day.

O God in Jesus Christ,
we gather into prayer all those who are lonely or lost today –
those for whom Christmas is painful or sad,
who dread the joy of others
with its comment on what they do not have.
Hold all people close to your heart this day, O God.

* * *

First Sunday after Christmas Day

LECTIONARY READINGS
Isaiah 61:10—62:3
Psalm 148
Galatians 4:4–7
Luke 2:22–40

One: Praise God, angels in heaven;
praise God, you creatures of earth!
Two: Praise God, sun and moon;
praise God, all you shining stars!
All: **Celebrate Emmanuel!**

One: Praise God, rushing waters;
praise God, you fish in the sea!
Two: Praise God, fire and hail;
praise God, you snow and frost!
All: **Celebrate Emmanuel!**

One: Praise God, animals and cattle;
praise God, you creeping things and flying birds!
Two: Praise God, young men and women;
praise God, old and young together!
All: **Celebrate Emmanuel!**
(from Psalm 148)

* * *

God of all the earth,
of sun and moon, mountains and hills,
wild animals and sea monsters,
fruit trees and scrub brush,
cedars and gum trees,
fire and frost,
people of all races and places,
old and young alike.

In this holy season
all peoples of the earth give you praise.
We ask your blessing on people of all faith communities
who celebrate with joy and delight
the feasts of faith in this season.
We especially remember in our community *(name the faith groups and feasts appropriate to your area).*
May we all know the blessing of your presence.
May you hear the varied voices of the earth sing your praise. Amen.

* * *

One: God of light and darkness, our world is in need of your presence. We, your people, long to experience you in all our being, with all our senses.
Two: Shine your light in us, O God,
All: **that we might shine for others.**
One: Help us not to stay focused on the infant Jesus in the manger or the temple, or the child that the magi visited. Help us instead to hear the message of the living Christ, who calls us to discipleship.
Two: Shine your light in us, O God,
All: **that we might shine for others.**
One: By your Spirit, guide us to take the message of unconditional love that is Christmas, and to share it with all the world, especially those who are in need, who are hurting, who are disillusioned, who have given up.
Two: Shine your light in us, O God,
All: **that we might shine for others.**
One: We pray in the name of Jesus:
Two: Child in the manger, Promise in the temple, Light for the nations.
All: **Amen.**

SEASON AFTER THE EPIPHANY

Epiphany of the Lord

LECTIONARY READINGS
Isaiah 60:1–6
Psalm 72:1–7, 10–14
Ephesians 3:1–12
Matthew 2:1–12

God, make us radiant, shining like beacons in the night that everyone who seeks peace and justice may gather and rejoice. Amen.

* * *

Thank you, Creator God, for the epiphanies you give us, generated from our recognition of your expansive and inclusive love for us, and for all creation. Teach us to serve you and one another as wise ones following the direction of your light. Amen.

* * *

Prepare us, O God, to welcome the events and people that mark turning points in our lives. Stir our imaginations to honour the dreams that send us in new directions. Give us courage to follow Christ's call to take another road. Amen.

* * *

As the wise ones sought Jesus by following a star,
let us follow the star-child
in the Christ-light of peace.
Holy light of God, shine on us.

As the wise ones dared to trust
in the wonders of the sky,

let us walk in the ways of compassion together
in the wonder of true community on earth.
Holy light of God, shine on us.

As the wise ones returned
to their country by another road,
let us travel a new path to justice and kindness.
Holy light of God, shine on us.

* * *

O Shining Light, we give thanks
for the light of this day,
for the light of eternal love,
for the light of the journey to justice and peace,
and for the light of your grace in our lives.
Shine through us, we pray,
that the light of joy may spread
through the world. Amen.

* * *

Let us go now by another road –
    the road of constant trust and faithfulness to God.
Let us be watchful –
    for those whose way is fearful;
let us be ready –
    to stand beside the outcast;
let us be prepared –
    to stay the course with those who suffer.
Let us go to the world
in the power of the Spirit
to fulfill our high calling as disciples of Christ,
who shines on us now and forever. Amen.

First Sunday after the Epiphany

Baptism of Jesus

LECTIONARY READINGS
Genesis 1:1–5
Psalm 29
Acts 19:1–7
Mark 1:4–11

God of power and of love, at his baptism you called Jesus your beloved son and sent your Spirit upon him. May we, born of water and of the Spirit, know ourselves to be beloved by you. Help us to rejoice in the new life to which you call us. Amen.

* * *

God of eternity,
whose spirit hovered over the waters of creation,
whose voice echoes down the rivers of history
and proclaims that we are your beloved children:
we gather here to worship you this day.
May we feel the power of your love
surrounding us and supporting us.
And when we leave this place
may we take your love and help it flow
in all of the arid places crying for
the refreshing presence of your Holy Spirit.
In the name of your beloved child, Jesus, we pray. Amen.

* * *

God of glory and strength,
too many times we act as though
we have been baptized with a baptism of repentance alone
never expecting nor wanting
the power that comes with forgiveness and your Spirit.
Forgive us for failing to lay claim to the new life Christ offers.

Help us move through repentance to rebirth.
Lay hold of us.
Let your glory thunder through our lives
like a voice over mighty waters.
Let the call of your Beloved echo in our souls.

*　*　*

Use an evergreen branch to sprinkle the people with water.
Here is the crossover point:
between Jesus the carpenter and Jesus the preacher;
between the private citizen and the public ministry;
between the "what ifs?" and the "now whats?"

Here is the crossover point:
through the water of that auspicious river;
through the ancient prophecies and the baptizer;
through the hopes and longings of the people of God.

Here is the crossover point:
and do we stand and watch,
or do we find our feet in the water
hearing that voice within us that says:
"I love you." I am with you. You are mine"?

*　*　*

In water
renew us.
In calling,
affirm us.
In living,
guide us.
In proclaiming,
strengthen us.
In faith,
encourage us.
In trusting,
love us.

Second Sunday after the Epiphany

LECTIONARY READINGS
1 Samuel 3:1–10, (11–20)
Psalm 139:1–6, 13–18
1 Corinthians 6:12–20
John 1:43–51

O God, you are constantly present in our lives and in the world, like a lamp burning through the night. Reveal yourself to us and through us. Tune our hearts and minds to recognize your bright calling to us to live in ways that reflect your steadfast love. Amen.

* * *

Before anything was,
God dreamed of me.
God searches for me,
God finds me.
Before I speak,
God hears me.
Before I move,
God is before me.
Before I was born,
God knew me.
Before I was seen,
God saw me.
Before I was named,
God called me.
Before I give praise,
God calls me here.

* * *

Here, in your presence,
may we hear you call our names
and willingly follow you.

So call us again, O God,
for we come with a desire
to know you better,
here and in every place you wait for us.

* * *

God of night-whispered wisdom,
forgive us for the times
we fail to seek your will or heed your call.
Forgive us when we fail to act on the truth we know,
the knowledge we have, the possibility there is for change.
Forgive us when we let our love
for family or friends or church or nation
blind us to their faults – and ours.

Know that you are forgiven and freed to forgive others.
Walk into a future shaped not by failures,
but by God's justice and mercy. Amen.

* * *

Gracious God,
may we imagine your vision for all your people:
the lonely who need a friend,
the hungry who need food,
the homeless who need shelter,
the sick and weary who need a bed,
those who can't rest because there's too much to do,
those who would like to feel useful, too.

We pray too for creation –
the animals and the plants –
and imagine a future
that looks like a joyful dance.

We thank you, God, for calling to us,
for calling us into the future with you.
May we hear, understand, imagine, and follow,
and live into your vision for all. Amen.

*　*　*

Based on Psalm 139

Teach response before beginning prayer.
Many, many years ago people wrote songs about God's great love for us. The people were so happy, they wanted to sing about it and dance about it. (*Can add the following sentence and then blow bubbles before the response if desired.* [If they could, they might have even wanted to blow bubbles about God's love.]) This is a song one person wrote about God's love.

O God, you are always with me.
I am never alone.
And you know me, and you love me (*bubbles*)
here and there, always and everywhere.

Oh God, you know what I am doing.
You know what I am thinking – even before I say it.
And you know me, and you love me (*bubbles*)
here and there, always and everywhere.

You are great, God, so great and kind and caring.
You have given me the gift of family and friends.
And you know me, and you love me (*bubbles*)
here and there, always and everywhere.

O God, your love is big!
Wherever I go, your love is there.
Your love surrounds me like a blanket.
And you know me, and you love me (*bubbles*)
here and there, always and everywhere.

Third Sunday after the Epiphany

LECTIONARY READINGS
Jonah 3:1–5, 10
Psalm 62:5–12
1 Corinthians 7:29–31
Mark 1:14–20

You seek us, Holy One, to be participants in the building of your reign on earth. When we hear your call we sometimes respond with "I can't" resounding in our hearts. May we remember, always, that with your call comes the promise of you being with us always. Amen.

* * *

God of mercy,
in each second of time you are with us:
you call us to discipleship,
you invite us into relationship one with another
and with you, our Creator.
In the moments of this worship
may we experience your call,
your community, your grace,
and be led to respond. Amen.

* * *

The God who calls us
speaks into our uncertainties,
calls us to follow
even when we aren't so sure.
God continues to call,
and to our reluctant hearts says,
"It is enough for now.
Come follow me. You are ready."

* * *

Loving God,
we live in a world that is ever-changing.
Yet your love remains constant.
We give up on you,
and on ourselves, sometimes –
but you do not give up on us.
We thank you for calling us
to be prophets, disciples, and ministers.
Sometimes we answer quickly,
and sometimes slowly,
yet in all times, you accept us.
We pray this day for all who hear your call
and who respond.
Help us to embody your compassion for all creation
in all we do.
When we say "yes" quickly,
channel our enthusiasm to do your work.
When we say "no,"
don't give up on us, but guide us back.
When we give up, get overwhelmed,
burnt out, discouraged,
give us rest and energy to carry on.
We pray also for those
whose call is not affirmed
and whose response is silenced.
Hear their lament,
and give their ministry voice and vision.
Fill us with your spirit
that we may speak your word,
love your people,
and care for your creation without limits.
We pray in Jesus' name. Amen.

* * *

O God, we long for your way of justice
and we are willing to follow you
as you journey into places of injustice
(*offer specific petitions*).

O God, we long for peace to prevail
and we are willing to follow you
as you journey into places of conflict
(*offer specific petitions*).

O God, we long to know your healing
and we are willing to follow you
as you journey into places of dis-ease and pain
(*offer specific petitions*).

O God, we long for your way in this world
and we are willing to follow you
as you journey into new and unknown places
in order to share the love of God
(*offer specific petitions*).

* * *

As Jonah moved from whale belly to town crier,
from runaway to prophet,
we will move from where we are,
to where you will take us.

As Peter and Andrew moved from shoreline to preaching,
from net-menders to disciples,
we will move from our routine
into your surprises.

As James and John moved
from boat builders to apostles,
from habit to adventure,
we will move from what is known
into what is unknown.

Fourth Sunday after the Epiphany

LECTIONARY READINGS
Deuteronomy 18:15–20
Psalm 111
1 Corinthians 8:1–13
Mark 1:21–28

Powerful God, make us bold to embrace your wisdom and be shaped by its way. Speak to us that we might enact your word and transform our world in amazing ways to conform to your way of compassion, love, and justice. Amen.

* * *

Leader could point to various body parts mentioned and invite congregation to join in. Works best if people do not need to focus on reading (that is, project prayer or one voice reads).

Dear God,
open our *ears* to hear what you are saying to us today.
Open our *eyes*, to see where Jesus' healing love is needed in our world.
Open our *hands*, to do your work and help where help is needed.
Open our *lips*, to bring comfort, joy, and laughter to your people.
Open our *minds*, to hear new truths about how you work in our world.
Open our *hearts*, to love you, our neighbours, and ourselves as you love us. Amen.

* * *

God of deserving praise,
you gift us with voices to witness,
hands to extend in welcome and care,
and hearts to love.
May your calling grow deeper within us
as your Spirit equips and inspires us
with power to do your will.

* * *

One: We pray with those who long for a message of hope:
All: **may we be the hopeful Body of Christ.**

One: We pray with those who long for a healing touch:
All: **may we be the healing Body of Christ.**

One: We pray with those who yearn for freedom:
All: **may we be the liberating Body of Christ.**

One: We pray with those who seek a return to community:
All: **may we be the reconciling Body of Christ.**

One: We pray with those who would like to know you more, O God.
All: **May we be the Body of Christ bearing witness to your loving presence in the world. Amen.**

* * *

May God, who is love, hold you.
May God, who is liberation, free you.
May God, who is healing, restore you to wholeness.
May we who have celebrated the gift of Christ's teaching and healing, go from this place to be a people that lives and teaches God's reconciling love in the world. Amen.

* * *

When our spirits are troubled, God brings us peace.

When our spirits are hurting,
God is our source of healing.

When our spirits falter,
God gives us strength to carry on.

When our spirits alienate us from others,
God reconciles us to community.

In God who is peace and healing,
strength and reconciling love, we trust. Amen.

Fifth Sunday after the Epiphany

LECTIONARY READINGS
Isaiah 40:21–31
Psalm 147:1–11, 20c
1 Corinthians 9:16–23
Mark 1:29–39

O God, our strength, lift us up on wings as a mother eagle supporting her young. When we are weary, restore us to your purpose and fill us with your hope. Amen.

* * *

Grant to us, O God,
to know that which is worth knowing,
to love that which is worth loving,
to praise that which pleases you most,
to respect that which is most precious to you,
and to dislike whatever is evil in your eyes.
Grant us the judgment to distinguish things that differ,
and above all to search out and do
the things that are most pleasing to you,
through Jesus Christ our Lord. Amen.
Thomas à Kempis, 15th century

* * *

We confess to you, O God,
the moments when we do not trust your presence
or our own sense of it.
We confess, too,
those moments when we pretend we know all things
and are in control of everything.
And we confess
those moments when we think we can hide
our thoughts and our actions from you.
Forgive us, we pray, in Jesus' name. Amen.

* * *

In the book of Isaiah we read that all who wait upon God will find a new and wondrous strength: they will run and not be weary, walk and not faint, and even soar with eagles. So may we find our own faith and strength renewed, as we find ourselves forgiven by our loving God.

* * *

Weakness and exhaustion are facts of life
and even the young grow tired.
But those who wait on God,
the source of eternal strength,
will be renewed body and soul.
When the Spirit of God lifts us up
we will be like eagles rising in the sky,
like marathon runners at peak performance
giving our all in service to God.

* * *

May God who calls you into stillness sustain you.
May Jesus who shows you a way of balance and peace travel with you.
May the Spirit give you rest, and refresh you for your journey until you return.

* * *

May the Christ who walks on wounded feet
    walk with you on the road.
May the Christ who serves with wounded hands
    stretch out your hands to serve.
May the Christ who loves with a wounded heart
    open your hearts to love.
May you see the face of Christ in everyone you meet
    and may everyone you meet
    see the face of Christ in you.

Traditional Celtic prayer

Sixth Sunday after the Epiphany

Proper 1. If this is the Sunday before Ash Wednesday, this Proper may be replaced by the readings for the last Sunday after the Epiphany, Transfiguration Sunday.

LECTIONARY READINGS
2 Kings 5:1–14
Psalm 30
1 Corinthians 9:24–27
Mark 1:40–45

Invite congregation to join in the actions. Can also be used as prayer of confession by inviting the people to respond, "Forgive us God" after each of the first three statements.

(Cover eyes.) Sometimes, God, we do not recognize you in the faces of those around us.
(Cover ears.) Sometimes we do not want to listen to the advice of others, or hear your word proclaimed in ways that might challenge us.
(Fold arms across chest and assume stubborn facial expression.) We can be stubborn, thinking we know everything and refusing to learn new ways and ideas.
(Relax, unfold arms, and hold them out, palms up.) Open us, God, to your word and your love, moving and living in our world. Help us to celebrate your presence in others, and to respond to your invitation to live and act in new ways. Amen.

* * *

Loving God,
we thank you for the many psalms and stories that tell us of the turning of life's seasons:
joy will follow sorrow as
warming springtime follows winter
and cooling autumn follows summer.

We thank you for being with us in all the seasons of our lives,
a steady presence
bringing peace in the midst of the changes we must face.
We gladly sing praises to you, Maker of heaven and earth. Amen.

* * *

Today is a day of possibility.
God whispers the call to you,
"Welcome!"
We come with little,
God comes with all that is.
We come as strangers and wanderers,
God welcomes us to the family of God.
In this moment,
in this place,
we will experience the touch of God.
Come, you are welcome here.

* * *

The gifts of God come to us in an open hand.
They are given gently and quietly,
but we are a people of clamour and noise
and your gifts, O God, so often wait for us in vain.
At every moment you reach out to touch us
in the very heart of our being.
Yet we so often prefer our own pain and confusion.
For all the moments that we have missed your touch,
for all the days we have not experienced your willing and giving love,
for all the times we have lived as if we did not need you,
for all of this, we offer our sorrow,
and we wait in confidence for your healing touch.
(time for silent reflection)
Creatures of earth, people of heaven,
hear the word of God:
because of the life, death, and resurrection of Jesus
you are now of the company of the forgiven.
Thanks be to God!

* * *

Use this guided meditation to lead people in prayer.

Imagine you have an adhesive bandage on your hand. See this healing tool and recognize the healing power it contains. It will bring comfort. It will prevent infection. It will keep painful objects from the wound.

Now imagine that you can place this bandage over a part of our world that is in pain. It may be a nation or a group of people. It may be some part of our environment. Think of that place now and pray for God's healing power…

Imagine yourself putting the bandage on a group or relationship of which you are a part. Where is the interpersonal struggle God is revealing to you now? See God touch this area of your life and pray for healing…

Finally, if you were to put the bandage on a part of your body that represents a place in need of healing, where would that be? It might be physical, emotional, or spiritual. Imagine yourself putting the bandage on this spot and pray again for God's healing power…

* * *

To one who is ill Jesus said:
I choose to make you well.
To those who suffer in our world,
God says: You are my beloved ones;
know that I am with you
and your suffering will not last forever.
To the places of pain in our lives,
God says: You may weep now
but joy will come in the morning.
May God's healing touch cover us
and comfort us in this time and always.

* * *

Distribute adhesive bandages to everyone in the congregation and invite them to place it on one of their fingers and to leave it on as long as they can. Let it be a reminder of the healing they receive from God and the healing they can bring to others.

The hand of God is at work in all the world at all times.
We are invited to be hands of God,
to bring healing,
to bring hope,
to touch the world.
Go in peace and gratitude.
Thanks be to God. Amen.

Seventh Sunday after the Epiphany

Proper 2. If this is the Sunday before Ash Wednesday, this Proper may be replaced by the readings for the Last Sunday after the Epiphany, Transfiguration Sunday.

LECTIONARY READINGS
Isaiah 43:18–25
Psalm 41
2 Corinthians 1:18–22
Mark 2:1–12

Merciful and compassionate God, we lay our lives before you, seeking your gifts of forgiveness and new life. Free us and guide us so that our friendships may be expressions of the love you have for all of us. Amen.

* * *

Teach us, O God, to let go of the past and to look to you to do a "new thing." Help us to free ourselves and one another through forgiveness and compassion, that our relationships may be expressions of and responsive to the love you have for all of us. Amen.

* * *

One:	God provided water in the desert and streams in the wasteland.
Left side:	God heals the sick.
Right side:	God forgives sin.
Leader:	God has formed us for God's self.
Left side:	God remembers sin no more.
Right side:	God delivers us in times of trouble.
Left side:	God has mercy on everyone.
Right side:	God is faithful.

Left side: God puts the Spirit in our hearts.
Right side: God loves all the world.

Leader: God says, "Yes" to the world.
Left side: God says, "Yes" to the world.
Right side: God says, "Yes" to the world.

All: *(shout)* **Yes!**

* * *

God of love and forgiveness,
God of life and wholeness,
in Jesus you say "yes" to us:
yes to new beginnings,
yes to our dreams,
yes to hope and healing.
May we say "yes" to you
in our words, thoughts, and actions,
this day and always. Amen.

* * *

O God,
you made the whole universe in gladness and joy,
and in every new day you renew all of creation.
Everything that is, is a gift from you.
Why then do we, the people of your earth, the inheritors of your boundless generosity,
so often live our lives in fear,
in mean-spiritedness, and in shame?
We are the people of your promise,
we need to hear your forgiving word.
We need to feel your healing touch.
We need to see the new thing
that even now is springing up.
(*Allow time for silent reflection.*)

* * *

God, who hears every prayer and knows every thought,
says to us, "Forget the former things;
do not dwell on the past.
See, I am doing a new thing!
Now it springs up."
Know that you are forgiven.
Thanks be to God.

Last Sunday after the Epiphany

Transfiguration Sunday

LECTIONARY READINGS
2 Kings 2:1–12
Psalm 50:1–6
2 Corinthians 4:3–6
Mark 9:2–9

We climb mountains seeking you, God,
but not knowing quite what we are looking for.
Your presence appears as a voice from the clouds,
bright as dazzling light,
as incomprehensible mystery,
the extraordinary breaking through into the ordinary,
and we are touched by the holy.
In these high places,
in the thin places,
we see, we hear, we know you, God –
closer, deeper, beyond imagining,
beyond expressing.

Take us to the thin places.
Lead us to moments of epiphany, revelation.
Guide us to thin places
where holiness touches ordinariness,
and where we long to see you
face to face. Amen.

* * *

God of light and glory,
may we recognize your glory around us –
a sense of the sacred found in the everyday:
in the stories of faith we tell,
in the lives of the people we meet,

in the words we use to speak.
May your majesty and mystery
always be within our seeing,
close enough for our hearing,
and present in our living.

* * *

Invite people to sit with their hands clenched in a fist, their arms tucked tightly in front of them, and their heads bowed. Following the prayer, play instrumental music and give people time to unclench their fists, unfold their arms, lift their heads, and slowly stand.

God of the mountains and clear skies,
here we can see ourselves more clearly,
where the air is thinner and the light is clearer,
and we confess we long to fold up our living.
We long to hide away from the times
when what we have done
has not brought glory to you
and has caused you and others pain.
We want to forget those times
when the opportunities for doing what is right
have not been taken,
and the chance to speak out
has not been grasped.
We want to fold up,
hide from the truth,
and be left alone.
(moment of silence)

But you are the God of transformation.
Transfigure our confession,
that we may hear your forgiveness,
and find renewal and life again.
(*Play music as people unfold and stand.*)

* * *

Our God, God of tender mercies,
we pray for the world –
this grand and sad place,
this place of wonder and pain.
We pray for our families,
especially for those who are yet to experience
your gentle healing touch.
We pray for our community that together
we will live out the true meaning of our call.
We pray for our nation,
for the gap between the grand story we tell of ourselves
and the reality we so often see.
Give us a vision of a new world.
We pray for those places
where the pain and suffering is more than we can "comprehend."
We pray as your people,
as those who have glimpsed something
of what your presence can mean.
We pray for your glory to cover the earth
like the sky that blankets everything. Amen.

* * *

Not on the mountaintop,
but into the world
we will take a sense of the sacred.
Not in the memorialized story,
but in the work of today
we will live a sense of the sacred.
We go to let the glory out
and to bring the love of Jesus
into the world and transfigure it.

SEASON OF LENT

Lent 1

LECTIONARY READINGS
Genesis 9:8–17
Psalm 25:1–10
1 Peter 3:18–22
Mark 1:9–15

Teach us your paths, O God, and lead us in your truth. You have been steadfast in your love for us, and merciful in welcoming and sustaining us. Forgive us when we move away from your loving paths, and strengthen us to follow in your way. Amen.

* * *

Creator God, thank you for never failing to seek us and bless us through your promise of loving care. Open our hearts to see your word at work in our lives. Amen.

* * *

One: Here is the journey that moves beyond where we are now. Come, trust the God whose journey it is. Come, and trust in the steadfast love of God. This is Lent. This is the journey.
Two: Here is the journey, for all who long to travel. Come, for God makes known love's path, and invites us to follow, trusting in the steadfast love of God. This is Lent. This is the journey.
Three: Here is the journey, for all those who want to know truth. Come, this is the way of salvation, and we wait for God's call into steadfast love. This is Lent. This is the journey.
Four: Here is the journey that takes us further than we have been before. Come, for God leads the humble into what is right, surrounded by the steadfast love of God. This is Lent. This is the journey.

* * *

To you, O God, we lift up our souls,
and we will follow in your paths.
To you, O God, we lift up our souls,
and we will be led by your truth.
To you, O God, we lift up our souls,
and we will learn of forgiveness.
Your paths are steadfast love,
and we will travel in them forever.

* * *

God who makes rainbows,
we know we hang on to things that we shouldn't.
We can be scared to let go of our comforts, our riches, the things that make life easy for us.
Like Noah,
enable us to leave behind all the things that hold us back from setting out on the voyage to which you have called us.
Help us to pick up and carry with us the things that refresh our lives; hope, love, and renewal; our lives, homes, and our communities.

* * *

We come to you, O God,
in this Season of Lent,
to reflect again on Jesus' journey to the cross,
and beyond that to resurrection.
We dare to do that, supported by stories of the many promises and covenant you made to your people throughout history.
Come to us in this season, O God,
and remind us once again that you're always with us:
in death and resurrection,
in desert and in flood. Amen.

* * *

Place a large bowl of water at the front, or reposition the font if appropriate. After this liturgy, invite the congregation to move past the water (can sing an appropriate hymn or have music play), running their finger through it and drawing a symbol on themselves.

One:	This first day of Lent is a reminder of God's rainbow promise to renew all creation, and a time to remember God's promise to us in our baptism.
Two:	Let us recall God's promises to us through water.
One:	This is water from God's world. It tells us about the promises God gives: to renew us, to forgive us, to lead us into unknown and undiscovered futures.
Two:	It is the water of baptism.
All:	**It is the water of life.**
One:	This is the water from God's world. It tells us about God's community: always creating, always inviting, always calling us into a life grounded in eternity.
Two:	It is the water of baptism.
All:	**It is the water of life.**
One:	This is water from God's world. It tells us about a time before memory: when God first loved us; when God first spoke our names; when God first introduced us; calling us to follow Jesus through the waters.
Two:	It is the water of baptism.
All:	**It is the water of life.**
One:	Come now and renew the promise with the one who renews us.

* * *

As we journey, God says to you and me:
I am with you,
I hold you,
I call you,
I know you,
I care for you,
I travel with you,
I give myself to you,
I am on this journey with you,
I am God, and my steadfast love is with you always.
Let us travel in peace.

* * *

Lent 2

LECTIONARY READINGS
Genesis 17:1–7, 15–16
Psalm 22:23–31
Romans 4:13–25
Mark 8:31–38 **or** Mark 9:2–9

God, we give thanks that you call each of us by name and offer the gift of life lived in your presence. Send your Spirit to guide us as we respond with faith to your call and live with trust in your promise. Amen.

* * *

Whisper your name.
Hear its sound, feel its rhythm, recognize its worth
and know the one who spoke it long before anyone else did.
It is unique to you – your very own.
Its sound is a promise whispered among the stars,
first spoken when the universe was unfolded.
And there it is engraved, one among a billion galaxies:
God's covenant for every future,
wrapped up in your name.
Whisper it.
Hear its sound.
Feel its rhythm.
Recognize its worth.
And hear it on the lips of the one whose promise it is.

* * *

We come to you, O God, for you do not turn away.
We come to you, O God, for you have heard our cry.
We come to you, O God, for you live in us.
May this time be sacred,
shaped beyond this world,
and ready for encounter.
We come to you, O God, for you come to us in Jesus.

* * *

Prayer of confession

Invite five people to read the following monologues. After each, the reader pauses and turns his or her back on the congregation for the remainder of the prayer.

One: Time! There's not enough of it. Who has the energy to care about homelessness, asylum seekers, or the stranger? Everyone should have a home, but…

Leader: God forgive us when we turn away from the homeless and the work of finding a home for everyone.

**All: You are with the homeless;
may we follow you there.**

Two: It's too hard to face. Who doesn't feel helpless in the face of illness? We want to fill up the uncomfortable silence, yet we cannot find a useful word. Everyone should be visited, but…

Leader: God forgive us when we allow our discomfort to distance us from others.

**All: You are with the sick and dying;
may we follow you there.**

Three: War is someone else's business – politicians, activists, soldiers – someone else, anyone else. Who understands what's going on anyway? Even if we did, what could we do about it? We know war only leads to destruction, but…

Leader: God forgive us when we keep silent when you want us to speak peace.

**All: You are with those who make peace;
may we follow you there.**

Four: Hunger and poverty are very real in our world and we know your heart grieves. But who can make a difference anyway? Who knows if the resources get to the right people? We know compassion is central to who we are as people, but…

Leader: God forgive us when our ears become deaf to the needs around us.

**All: You stand with those in need;
may we follow you there.**

Five: Every day we see the effects of climate change and our neglect of the earth. It is easy to point our fingers at the big industries and other countries who are not doing enough to care for the environment. We know you have called us to be good stewards of your creation, but…

Leader: God forgive us when we call on others to change, and forget about our own responsibilities.

All: **You are at home in the heart of creation; may we follow you there.**

* * *

When we follow the world,
God turns us towards the promise.
When we move towards old age,
God moves us towards a new age.
When we prepare to settle down,
God prepares to unsettle us.
When we organize our retirement,
God organizes more adventures.
When we sort out our pension,
God sorts out our travel plans.
When we wonder if we get lost in the crowd,
God knows each of us by name.
So go: know that God goes before you,
and is beside you in all of your travels. Amen.

* * *

Lent 3

LECTIONARY READINGS
Exodus 20:1–17
Psalm 19
1 Corinthians 1:18–25
John 2:13–22

Wise and loving God, strengthen our willingness to listen to your words of wisdom and live by them. Strengthen our faith to live as children blessed by your promise of new life. Amen.

∗ ∗ ∗

The heavens sing out your glory, O God, and your grace shines new each day. Help us live out such grace in our harmony with one another, and experience again the wonder of your presence in every person we encounter; in Jesus the Christ. Amen.

∗ ∗ ∗

Great God,
may our voices join the heavens
as we proclaim your call for justice.
May we recognize the abundance of the earth,
and call for equal share among all your creatures.
May we meet you in this place of glory,
as we join you on the way to Jerusalem.
May we celebrate all you have done for us,
and meet you in the suffering of life.

∗ ∗ ∗

The great wonder of God
is God's forgiveness,
yet it never leaves us the same.
Like creases and folds,
our living scars the surface of our lives,

giving shape to
relationships, community, and creation.
This is the person God loves completely
and gives everything for.
This is the true wonder of God.

* * *

Prayer
In the places where everything becomes a "god," we pray for discernment.
Help us, God.
In the places where "God" is an oppressive word, we pray for liberation.
Help us, God.
In the places where God cannot be worshipped, we pray for freedom.
Help us, God.
In the places where children reject parents and parents reject children, we pray for love.
Help us, God.
In the places where life is devalued, we pray for reverence.
Help us, God.
In the places where others' gifts have no value, we pray for deference.
Help us, God.
In the places where there is deceit, we pray for honesty.
Help us, God.
In the places where there is envy, we pray for respect.
Help us, God. Amen.

* * *

God's living way is before us,
and we will move towards it.
God's place of justice is beside us,
and we will wait here with the forgotten.
God's call for renewal is within us,
and we will respond without counting the cost.

* * *

Lent 4

LECTIONARY READINGS
Numbers 21:4–9
Psalm 107:1–3, 17–22
Ephesians 2:1–10
John 3:14–21

Loving God, we thank you and rejoice in our wholeness through the Spirit. May we show our thanks as we work for wholeness in all creation, beginning with the last and the least, just as you chose to do; in Jesus the Christ. Amen.

* * *

Sometimes we feel like wanderers in the wilderness, O God,
not sure which way to turn
and feeling lost and alone.
Help us to remember even the wilderness,
even the desert,
can be a place
of life and healing,
and that with you
we can face our fears.
Help us to remember that you are always with us.
We pray in Jesus' name. Amen.

* * *

Gather us in from the lands, loving God:
from the east and from the west,
from the north and from the south.
Gather us in from other lands and other waters.
Be with us here in this moment,
and in all places where we go. Amen.

* * *

Imagine yourself alone at this table, spread with simple food.
Imagine you are praying before you eat.
For what do you give thanks in your life at this time?
(Pause.)
What feels unresolved or unsettled in your life at this time?
(Pause.)
What relationships may need your renewed attention?
(Pause.)
What healing would you like to hear right now?
(Pause.)
When you feel ready, finish your time of prayer.

* * *

Come all who need justice,
God weaves in us the path of life.
Come all who need peace,
God weaves in us the way of truth.
Come all who need comfort,
God weaves in us a sure hope.
Come all who need healing,
God weaves in us the promise of wholeness.
Come all who need community,
God weaves in us the love of Christ.
Come all who need God,
God weaves us in the heart of the Divine.
Give thanks to God for God is good.
God's steadfast love endures for all time.

* * *

I am not alone.
I know a presence around me,
in the air I breathe within me,
in the sounds I hear beyond me,
and know their source
streams from the great love
that brings and blesses all life,
always there,
streaming from the birthplace of all things.
I am not alone.
I am loved by Love itself,
that will never let go.
I move in its delicious vastness.
I am a drifter.
Give thanks to God for God is good.
God's steadfast love endures for all time.

Lent 5

LECTIONARY READINGS
Jeremiah 31:31–34
Psalm 51:1–12 **or** Psalm 119:9–16
Hebrews 5:5–10
John 12:20–33

Create in us clean hearts, O God. Fill us with your Spirit, that we may find joy and gladness in your presence. Amen.

* * *

One: Seek. Declare. Treasure. Delight. Meditate.
Two: In our inward being, stir us, O God.
One: Wash. Purge.
Two: Create a clean heart within us, O God.
One: This is the time to begin anew.
Amen.

* * *

Have the sound of a heartbeat playing in the background. You can do this with a gentle drumbeat or with a CD of a heartbeat found at a baby supply store. Fade the sound out at the end of the prayer. Announce that when the leader says, "Hear us as we pray," the people will respond, "Create a new heart in me, O God."
At times our hearts are empty.
We expend all of our attention
at work, at school, at church, in community
until we have nothing left to give
and our inner beings feel like vacant shells.
Hear us as we pray:
Create a new heart in me, O God. *(silence)*
At times our hearts burn with resentment.
Life has been unfair

and we rehearse the dealings of our past
until forgiveness of ourselves and others is nearly impossible.
Hear us as we pray:
Create a new heart in me, O God. *(silence)*
At times our hearts are paralyzed with fear.
We wonder: Where is the safe and familiar?
How will we move forward?
What are we to do?
Hear us as we pray:
Create a new heart in me, O God. *(silence)*

* * *

God longs to place truth in our inner beings;
to make our hearts beat
with the love and justice of God's own heart.
With the dawning of each day,
God creates newness without and within
and our spirits are restored
with the joy of saving grace.
"You are my sacred one,"
is written on our hearts
so live now in this truth.

* * *

One: This is the path of life,
Two: among the shadows of the world,
One: finding the moments of hope,
Two: amid the rising of the cross.
One: May our hands cup the grain,
Two: our lives bear the faith,
One: our souls grip the truth,
Two: our hearts trust the promise.
All: **May God's steadfast love be our travelling companion.**
One: May we enjoy a lifetime seeking God,
Two: who does not hide from us,

One:	but lives with us through all suffering,
Two:	and bears us into wholeness.
All:	**May God's presence always be our travelling companion.**
One:	May we move out onto the way
Two:	and with truth and righteousness,
One:	celebrate our living in God,
Two:	in every place around and within.
All:	**May the cry of heaven always be our travelling companion.**
One:	May we live in thanks to God,
Two:	for the love that endures all things,
One:	hearing the promise of wholeness,
Two:	in all the world's brokenness.
All:	**May provision of grace always be our travelling companion.**
One:	May we hear the beating of a new heart,
Two:	inscribed with God's loving law,
One:	a law of justice and righteousness,
Two:	a law of love and fairness for all.
All:	**May we live in covenant with the one we call God.**

* * *

All:	**We go to listen for God,**
Leader:	speaking in every heartbeat!
All:	**We go to serve God,**
Leader:	whose law is written on our hearts!
All:	**We go in the presence of God,**
Leader:	who has declared that only a heartbeat away is the promise of resurrection.
All:	**Thanks be to God. Amen.**

* * *

One:	As we leave this time and place, we go out in good heart to
Two:	seek.
Three:	Declare.
Two:	Treasure.
Three:	Delight.
Two:	Meditate.
One:	As we leave this time and place, we go out in good heart to
Two:	face the needs of this hour
Three:	and bear the fruit of love in the world.
All:	**This is the time to begin anew.**

* * *

Lent 6

Palm/Passion Sunday

LECTIONARY READINGS
(*for the Liturgy of the Palms*)
Mark 11:1–11 **or** John 12:12–16
Psalm 118:1–2, 19–29

(*for the Liturgy of the Passion*)
Isaiah 50:4–9a
Psalm 31:9–16
Philippians 2:5–11
Mark 14:1—15:47 or Mark 15:1–39, (40–47)

Deep Spirit, present within all things,
we gather as a people, alive with hopes, fears, longings, joy, and weariness.
We come in worship,
we come in community,
we come in expectant vulnerability.
In peace, may we continue our journey from Lent into Holy Week.
May worship be filled with a sense of wonder, a sense of fragile longing about the events to come, a sense of what it means to be part of our sacred humanity. In the spirit of Jesus we pray.
Amen.

* * *

Give thanks to God
for God's love remains steadfast and true.

Though the future is uncertain
and the way is dimmed by threat of violence

we give thanks to God
for God's love remains steadfast and true.

Even as hatred barricades the road
our love leads us on
and we give thanks to God
for God's love remains steadfast and true.

We lay down our lives and lift up our praise
for the one who comes in God's name to save
and we give thanks to God
for God's love remains steadfast and true.

* * *

Blessed Hosannah,
who saves us with love,
draw close to us on this day.
Remind us that you are with us always,
in all moods and seasons,
in all our doubts and fears.

May we draw close to you at this time –
after the palm branches have withered
and the songs of praise have died away –
may our love for you remain steadfast and true.

* * *

Brother Christ,
help us to follow you
deep into the waters of baptism,
to break the chain of past wrongs,
to become fit to face your coming age.
Jesus, our Brother, help us to follow you.
Help us to follow you into the desert,
with you to fast, denying false luxury-values,
refusing the tempting ways of self-indulgence,

the way of success at all costs,
the way of coercive persuasion.
Jesus, our Brother, help us to follow you.
Help us to follow you in untiring ministry
to town and village,
to heal and restore,
to cast out the demonic forces
of greed, resentment, communal hatred,
and self-destructive fears rampant in our lands.
Jesus, our Brother, help us to follow you.
Help us to follow you into the place of quiet retreat,
to intercede for the confused, the despairing, the anxiety-driven,
to prepare ourselves for costly service.
Jesus, our Brother, help us to follow you.
Help us to follow you on the road to Jerusalem,
to set our faces firmly against friendly suggestions
to live a sage, expedient life,
to embrace boldly the way of self-offering.
Jesus, our Brother, help us to follow you.
Help us to follow you even to the cross,
to see our hope in your self-spending love,
to die to all within us not born of your love.
Jesus, our Brother, help us to follow you.

Help us to follow you out of the dark tomb,
to share daily in your resurrection life,
to be renewed daily in your image of love,
to serve daily as your new body
being broken for your world.
Jesus, our Brother, help us to follow you.
Adapted by Christopher Duraisingh, India "A Litany of the Disciples of the Servant," Morning Noon and Night, ed. John Carden, CMS 1976, in Bread of Tomorrow: Prayers for the Church Year *ed. by Janet Morley, pp. 64–65*

* * *

"But if you wish to know how things come about, desire not understanding; ask for grace not instruction, the groaning of prayer not diligent reading, the spouse not the teacher, God not man, darkness not clarity, not light but fire."

Hear us on our Easter journey, O God.

A journey through the knotted experience of shadows and light, of pain and joy, of friendship and betrayal. May we hold this story of Palm/Passion Sunday close to our hearts this week, having it teach us eternal truths of the human condition and God's eternal grace.

* * *

SEASON OF EASTER

Easter Sunday

LECTIONARY READINGS
Acts 10:34–43 **or** Isaiah 25:6–9
Psalm 118:1–2, 14–24
1 Corinthians 15:1–11 **or** Acts 10:34–43
John 20:1–18 **or** Mark 16:1–8

God, we thank you that at the centre of your gospel is the story of your continual presence with us. In the Resurrection you welcome everyone from everywhere, all of us invited to sit with you in peace and friendship. Amen.

* * *

The women went, and found the stone was rolled away.
Alleluia!
"Don't be afraid!"
Alleluia!
"Jesus is not here – he has been raised!"
Alleluia!
"Look, here is where the body was."
Alleluia!
"Go and tell the others: he has been raised!"
Alleluia!
"Jesus is going ahead of you."
Alleluia!
Christ is risen!
Alleluia!
"Christ is risen indeed!"
Alleluia!

* * *

Left: In the steadfast love of God,
Right: in the presence that never leaves us,
Left: in the glory of the heavens this morning,
Right: in the companionship no matter what,
Left: in the deepest moments of living,
Right: in facing the places of life and of death,
All: we have travelled together.
Left: From isolation to common ground,
Right: from burial to empty grave,
Left: from crucifixion to gardens,
Right: from torture to celebration,
Left: from dying to living,
Right: from grief to mystery,
Left: from heartache to fear,
All: we have travelled together.
Left: This is the path of life,
Right: from tomb to resurrection,
**All: now we travel new paths
in this morning of God's reign.**

* * *

As purple gives way to gold,
hear our prayers for times of suffering,
in a world that is unjust for too many.
May we live toward wholeness.
As thorns give way to crowns,
hear our prayers for oppression in our land
by trade that is imbalance.
May we live toward liberation for all.
As tombs give way to gardens,
hear our prayers for worries
that keep us from flourishing in your care.
May we live toward your shalom.
As yesterday gives way to tomorrow,
hear our prayers for the future
that holds too much uncertainty or loneliness.
May we live toward your vision.

* * *

One: The world is full of pain; there is no hope.
Two: Let us believe the reign of God is already here!
One: People are sick, wars continue, earthquakes and floods abound. There is no hope.
Two: Let us believe the reign of God is already here!
Let us be open to the ways of God in our world.
One: The earth and its scarce resources continue to be consumed. There is no hope.
Two: Let us believe the reign of God is already here!
Let us be open to the ways of God in our world!
Let us find ways to live out our justice cry!
One: Indigenous peoples are ignored, and deep reconciliation avoided. There is no hope.
Two: Let us believe the reign of God is already here!
Let us be open to the ways of God in our world!
Let us find ways to live out our justice cry!
Let us seek ways to nurture the earth and extend compassion to those in need around us.
One: (*Offer prayers specific to concerns of your community.*)
Two: Can there really be hope? Can there ever be a different way? How can this be?
One: Let us believe the reign of God is already here!
Let us be open to the ways of God in our world!
Let us find ways to live out our justice cry!
Let us seek ways to nurture the earth and extend compassion to those in need around us.

O God, may the empty tomb remind us of the unexpected ways that justice, compassion, and healing can be brought to the most difficult and troubling circumstances.
With the Spirit of Christ we hold these things open.
Amen.

* * *

May our faith find voice and shout,
Christ is risen!
May our souls find purpose and shout,
Christ is risen!
May our voices find faith and shout,
Christ is risen!
May our hearts find life and shout,
Christ is risen!

* * *

Second Sunday of Easter

LECTIONARY READINGS
Acts 4:32–35
Psalm 133
1 John 1:1—2:2
John 20:19–31

God, help us to understand and experience the resurrection of Jesus as a welcome to all of us into true community where all are accepted and offered a home. May we rejoice in that great gift. Amen.

* * *

Leader: Come! Bring your doubts, your hopes, your faith.
People: Christ is risen! Alleluia!
Leader: Come! Bring your questions, your wonderings, your misgivings.
People: Christ is risen! Alleluia!
Leader: Come! Bring your fear, your sorrow, your joy.
People: Christ is risen! Alleluia!
Leader: Come, let us worship God.
People: Christ is risen! Alleluia!
All: Christ is risen indeed! Alleluia!

* * *

Sometimes we hide behind locked doors
or in tombs of our own making,
preferring to stay in familiar places
of doom, gloom, self-pity, and fear,
rather than to venture out into the
new and uncertain dawn of resurrection.
Come to us, God.
Open our locked doors and hearts,
enter in,
dust us off, and make us new.
We long to be your Easter people,
to live and proclaim new life
with all our being. Amen.

* * *

God,
you make space for light,
taking those burdens that fill us:
the pain that pushes out joy;
the guilt that pushes out innocence;
the hurt that pushes out love;
and you forgive them.
You roll them away,
creating space for light.
Fill us with the space made by forgiveness,
and help us to face the future with you and your love,
resurrected.
Amen.

* * *

God of every mystery,
may we live in trust of the Spirit
and filled with a sense of adventure.
May we reach out with your questions,
and let them shape our faith.
May we be open to the Spirit
provoking us,
disturbing us in this worship space,
they we may hear the call, follow,
and be led into new life.

* * *

Invite people to do a simple breathing prayer with you. On the in breath, everyone says *(silently)* "Fill me with your Spirit" and on each out breath they say, "Let your Spirit work through me."

You could easily change the word *Spirit* to a word such as *love, forgiveness*, or *grace*, or you could say "Fill me with your Spirit of love/forgiveness/grace/justice…" Invite people to repeat the prayer several times.

* * *

Statement of faith – I do not believe

This could be led by several voices, or simply by one.

I do not believe God wills hunger and poverty for the planet's children.
I do not believe God organizes the death of anyone, young or old.
I do not believe God hates our questions and detests our doubts.
I do not believe God wishes us to accept everything without debate.
I do not believe God likes the status quo that denies people liberty and freedom.
I do not believe God is silent in the councils of government.
I do not believe God approves what we have done to religion.
I do not believe God speaks only through words.
I do not believe God can be understood only through the interpretation of scholars.
I do not believe God is limited by human description.
I do believe God loves us.
I do believe God loves us so much that death was crushed, and life began anew.
I do believe what I can grasp, and hold, and touch, and also what I cannot grasp but know deep within.
I have not seen the empty tomb, but I believe in the Risen Christ.
I believe. God, help my unbelief.
Amen.

* * *

Listen to God's breath within:
it is the stirring of belief.
Voice those questions and doubts:
it is the making of faith.
Touch those scars and feel those wounds:
it is the place of resurrection.
Let the breath of God sustain you
this day and forever.

* * *

Third Sunday of Easter

LECTIONARY READINGS
Acts 3:12–19
Psalm 4
1 John 3:1–7
Luke 24:36b–48

When our hearts stir with insecurity
and we do not recognize you among us, we remember,
you alone, O Sacred Peace, are safety.
When discomfort swarms without and within
and common words do not satisfy, we remember,
you alone, O Sacred Peace, are safety.
Come, and reveal your presence as bread is broke
and the peace is shared so we can remember,
you alone, O Sacred Peace, are safety.
For you have put gladness in our hearts
more than when grain and wine abound, and we remember,
you alone, O Sacred Peace, are safety.
We remember you, O Sacred Peace,
and we come to worship.

* * *

Arrange to have readers situated throughout the worship space. A single voice will respond with the words, "peace be with you," from his or her seat after the first stanza. Add voices each time as designated to respond in unison from their seats.

Gathered in around memories
of shared experience and broken bread
we recognize your presence
and we celebrate.
Between resurrection surprise and the gift of Spirit,
One: peace be with you.
Confused by lingering questions

of one whose story seems incomplete:
Who was this Jesus and what difference does he make?
We live with you in the questions.
Between resurrection surprise and the gift of Spirit,
Five: peace be with you.
Wondering what the future holds
and trembling in uncertainty
because of what is asked of us
we await the assurance of you who calls us.
Between resurrection surprise and the gift of the Spirit,
Ten: peace be with you.
In this between time, O God,
may we hear your words of peace anew
as we celebrate, live, and wait
to behold Christ among us.
Between resurrection surprise and the gift of Spirit,
Fifteen: peace be with you.

* * *

Leader: Loving God, when we are frightened and filled with doubts…
All: **open us to the gospel of peace.**
Leader: When we think we understand everything and our minds are closed to new teachings…
All: **open us to the gospel of peace.**
Leader: When we do not understand, and our fears turn into anger or mistrust…
All: **open us to the gospel of peace.**
Leader: When we want to hide behind laws, regulations, and traditions that can hurt and exclude…
All: **open us to the gospel of peace.**
Leader: As the risen Christ came to be with the disciples and show them new possibilities…
All: **open us to the gospel of peace. Amen.**

Fourth Sunday of Easter

LECTIONARY READINGS
Acts 4:5–12
Psalm 23
1 John 3:16–24
John 10:11–18

Good Shepherd, we offer grateful thanks for your loving care. Open our hearts and minds to the guiding of your Spirit in our lives. Amen.

* * *

God, loving shepherd,
caring companion,
you who are ever-present with us
in all of life's adventures:
we gather here to celebrate
our faith as Easter people.
We celebrate that you care for us
unconditionally,
and love us no matter what;
that you seek us out when we are lost
and teach us to care for one another
as you care for us.
Accept the praise we offer,
we pray in Christ's name. Amen.

* * *

Called by name
a contemporary reading
There is a silence among the stars;
an expectant waiting,
alive to the rumour that the almighty is, once more, going to speak.
It is said that the angels have been preparing for centuries, millennia,
eons for this very moment of sound.

Everything has been battened down;
the universe is holding on with a firm grip.

The voice that shaped creation
is going to speak again.
The heavens tremble in anticipation;
the voice of the creator is getting ready.
What beautiful fjord or mountain will be formed in the holy breath?
What unimaginable wonder will evolve in the resonance of the voice?
What indescribable marvel will be whispered into life?

There is stillness across the cosmos,
and the whole order
is brought to the edge of their celestial seats
for the utterance.
God's throat is cleared
(there is a rumbling,
there is a stirring).
Hearts beat a little faster.
The whole of life,
even in the deepest reaches,
holds tight.
The word is forming,
rising,
intensifying,
evolving.
It is a shadow surfacing,
a hope expanding,
a word emerging into something as yet unheard.
that glides and skates and soars across the universe
in greater beauty than ever before,
glowing in the love with which it was spoken,
and surrounded by the grace in which it was conceived,
is the forming of your…
…name.

* * *

On this day, loving God,
we think of you as a shepherd who cares for all the sheep,
big and tall, short and small,
the ones who behave and the ones who don't,
those who wander off and those who stay close by.
Loving shepherd,
you care for us all.
We think of mothers:
those who gave us birth,
those who have raised us and care for us still,
for "mother-hearted women" who make us feel special,
for aunties and grandmas and neighbours and friends,
and all the women who touch our lives.
Loving shepherd,
you care for us all.

We think, too, of those who are sorrowing today:
those who are missing their mothers or their children,
those who mourn their dead,
those who worry and wonder,
those who dream dreams that never come true.
Loving shepherd,
you care for us all.

On this day, loving God, we think of families.
In the Bible you remind us that
families come in all shapes and sizes –
couples with no children,
foster families and adoptive families,
extended families and birth families,
single people and groups of people who call themselves family –
all sharing their lives together.
Loving shepherd,
you care for us all.

∗ ∗ ∗

Loving Shepherd,
through the gift of gathered community
may we know your attentive care,
abundant beauty,
and the power of reconciliation.
We pause now and, in the silence,
we hear you call each of us by name
and are welcomed and enfolded by your love.
(Pause.)
Guide us, protect us, feed us, renew us, love us.
Amen.

* * *

You are the Good Shepherd
and we are your sheep.
We come in all shapes and sizes,
all colours, personalities, quirks, and possibilities.
In your generous welcome,
you open wide the gates of community
so all can gather in and know your love.
You gently remind us
that not all your people are present.
Some are absent because of health,
some because of other obligations,
and some have been kept out
intentionally and unintentionally.
Through your prophetic words
bring us back to your way of hospitality
where all are enfolded in love.

* * *

Fifth Sunday of Easter

LECTIONARY READINGS
Acts 8:26–40
Psalm 22:25–31
1 John 4:7–21
John 15:1–8

God, as the branches are connected to the vine in every way that is possible, so are we connected to you. As the vine is connected to the earth from which it receives life, so we, through you, are connected to all that you have created. May we always know this truth. Amen.

* * *

Loving God,
we come together to reconnect to you,
the source of love.
No one has ever seen God,
but here, connected to one another,
God lives in us.
Grafted again to the taproot of love in this time together,
we strengthen ourselves to reach out like branches bearing good fruit to the world.
Abide with us in this time, O God,
so that we will continue to abide in love now and always.
Amen.

* * *

One: The keeping of vines
is an ancient form of farming the land,
cherishing the grapes that form wine
rich in flavour and hospitality.
Two: Come to the vine-keeper, all those bear fruit
who abide in the one who abides in us.
One: Vines are made of grafted branches,
that are pruned and nurtured
to produce the best fruit.

Two: Come, those who abide in Jesus,
to bear much fruit for the realm of God.
One: Jesus took the vines of earth,
and blessed them as an image of the followers of God.
Two: Come, those who know
they can do nothing of their own,
but only as part of the vine and branches.

* * *

We praise you –
you who planted us in this life,
and eternally tend us as your own.
Graft us into your spirit
that we may be bound together,
and held and affirmed
as one community in your love.
Nourish us with your compassion
and prune us with your truth
until we are one people,
abiding always in you and growing in love.
Easter God, you are the vine-keeper,
and we praise you –
you who grafts us into yourself,
and calls us your own.
May we be your Easter people,
bearing the fruit of resurrection faith.

* * *

Go into the world and bear the fruit of love.
Find the places of lifelessness and bring renewal.
Be the branches and create the community of life.
Do it all through the power of Jesus.

* * *

When you find yourself lost and alone,
may you be comforted by God who created you
and whose beloved child you are.
Amen.
When dry winds parch your soul,
may you be refreshed by Jesus Christ, the living water.
Amen.
When you do not know where to turn,
may you be guided on sacred paths
by the gentle breath of God's Holy Spirit.
Amen.

Sixth Sunday of Easter

LECTIONARY READINGS
Acts 10:44–48
Psalm 98
1 John 5:1–6
John 15:9–17

God, your word says you make the rain to fall on the just and the unjust. All of us are refreshed by you, no one misses out, no one goes away thirsty. May we live in the great bounty of your love and acceptance. Amen.

* * *

O God, we open our mouths to praise you and you open our spirits to receive you. We open our minds to learn of your ways and you open our wills to obey you. We open our hands to serve you and you open our hearts to love you. We are open to your mystery, O God, make yourself known in us this day.

* * *

God, in Jesus Christ you have made love known to us
in new and wonderful ways,
and you call us to love one another.
Jesus calls us friends,
and calls us to be friends with one another.
Teach us to love.
Teach us to be friends.
We pray in the name of our friend, Jesus. Amen.

* * *

One: Hear the words of Jesus:
"This is my commandment, that you love one another as I have loved you."
In the silence, we reflect on our willingness to love.
Two: Loving God, open our hearts to love more freely, more fully.
Many: Lord, hear our prayer.
One: Hear the words of Jesus:
"No one has greater love than this, to lay down one's life for one's friend."
In the silence, we reflect on the limits of our love.
Two: Loving God, open our hearts to love more freely, more fully.
Many: Lord, hear our prayer.
One: Hear the words of Jesus:
"You are my friends if you do what I command you."
In the silence, we open our hearts to friendship with Jesus.
Two: Loving God, open our hearts to love more freely, more fully.
Many: Lord, hear our prayer.

* * *

O God, we offer our lives
and all that we are to serving you.
We dedicate ourselves to living
as your obedient servants
and seek to love you by following
all you have commanded.
In Christ, you offer us friendship;
a sacred gift that makes serving you a joy.
Therefore, we will serve you, O God,
as friends united by your Spirit.
(Lift hands in the air.)
And all the friends of God say **Amen.**

* * *

Seventh Sunday of Easter

LECTIONARY READINGS
Acts 1:15–17, 21–26
Psalm 1
1 John 5:9–13
John 17:6–19

God of all wisdom, give us visions of the life you intend for us. Make your ways our ways. Guide us in building a Spirit-led community that bears fruit which is pleasing to you and beneficial to our neighbours. Amen.

* * *

Leader: What do you do when you are left alone?
What do you do with that ball of crumpled emotion
when meaning and purpose disappear,
as the one you follow is taken,
and the love you have chased is torn away?
What do you do when you are left alone?
Voice 1: Remember the dream!
Voice 2: Transform the visions into actions!
Voice 3: Turn the talk into work!
Voice 4: Follow in the footsteps!
Voice 5: Hear the future calling you!
Voice 6: Grow into community!
Voice 7: Pursue the promptings of your soul!
Voice 8: Grow up and walk!
Voice 9: Let go and let's adventure!
Voice 10: Be the church!
All: **Amen.**

* * *

Jesus prayed a prayer for his followers, that they may be one.
What divisions must we lay aside?
(silence)
Jesus prayed a prayer for his followers, that they may be protected.
What must we do to guard and keep each other?
(silence)
Jesus prayed a prayer for his followers, that joy may be complete.
What holds us back from complete joy?
(silence)
Jesus prayed a prayer for his followers, that they may be sanctified in truth.
What truth do we need to hear today?
(silence)

* * *

All:	**God calls all of us to ministry.** **Give us your Spirit, God,** **to answer your call.**
Leader 1:	When our language oppresses and our stories are not told,
Leader 2:	give us your Spirit, God,
People:	**to answer your call.**
Leader 1:	Where authority binds rather than liberates.
Leader 2:	give us your Spirit, God,
People:	**to answer your call.**
Leader 1:	When we discern your voice and then go our own way,
Leader 2:	give us your Spirit, God,
People:	**to answer your call.**
Leader 1:	Where new directions are not even considered,
Leader 2:	give us your Spirit, God,
People:	**to answer your call.**
Leader 1:	Where children are seldom seen and never heard,
Leader 2:	give us your Spirit, God,
People:	**to answer your call.**
All:	**God calls all of us to ministry.** **Give us your Spirit, God, to answer your call.**

Pentecost Sunday

LECTIONARY READINGS
Acts 2:1–21 **or** Ezekiel 37:1–14
Psalm 104:24–34, 35b
Romans 8:22–27 **or** Acts 2:1–21
John 15:26-27, 6:4b–15

Voice 1: Spirit of Joy – come like the wind, swirling among us; fill us with enthusiasm, and energize us to do your work and your will (*red streamer enters, waves*).
All: **Thank you, God, for the Spirit of Joy!**
Voice 2: Spirit of Truth – come as the flame of Christ's light among us, shining in our hearts, our minds, our lives (*orange streamer enters*).
All: **Thank you, God, for the Spirit of Joy!**
Voice 3: Spirit of Life – come as the breath of life, pouring energy and power into our dry bones, rekindling those who are weary, that we may have life and know God (*yellow streamer enters*).
All: **Thank you, God, for the Spirit of Joy!**
Voice 4: Spirit of Hope – come from the four winds breathing upon all your people, that all creation may be renewed with hope (*green or second red streamer enters*).
All: **Thank you, God, for the Spirit of Joy!**
Voice 5: Spirit of Love – come as our Comforter and Consoler, so that all who are broken and wounded are healed, so that all who grieve may be consoled by the power of your love and grace (*blue or second orange streamer enters*).
All: **Thank you, God, for the Spirit of Joy!**
Voice 6: Spirit of Wisdom – come as a light of understanding, that diversity in all its forms may be respected and may be understood as something to cherish (*purple, indigo, or second yellow streamer enters*).
All: **Thank you, God, for the Spirit of Joy!**

Voice 7: Spirit of Peace – come as the winds of truth, that our hearts may be kindled by the passion for justice and peace (*violet, black, brown, white, or third red streamer enters*).
All: **Thank you, God, for the Spirit of Joy!**

* * *

We are the people of the dream-weaver:
who put wonder into fjords,
perfume into roses,
and colour into laughter.

We are the people of the justice-maker:
who finds the crack in every prejudice,
stirs discontent into the oppressed,
and puts voice in the throats of the silenced.

We are the people for the Spirit-guide:
who knows the meaning of adventure,
opens up the world to our imaginings,
and calls us into it.

We are the people of the world;
who know your voice,
recognize your hand,
and struggle to answer your call. Amen.

* * *

When we pray for peace, O God,
may our prayers not be of words but of actions.

When we pray for justice, O God,
may our prayer not be of words but of choices we make.

When we pray for food for all, O God,
may our prayer not be of words but commitment to others.

When we pray for a greener world, O God,
may our prayer not be of words, but the lifestyle we choose.

When we pray for the world, O God,
may our prayer not be of words, but how we live here.

**May we live in the Holy Spirit:
in the energy of life, in the power of truth,
and with the impatience of justice.**

* * *

The imagination that sees in things
a shape never seen before;
the discovery that hears a chord
in a song never heard before;
the truth that recognizes a cry
from a voice never noticed before.
This is the work of the Spirit
and we are filled with praise.

The vision that notices a word on the page
never understood before;
the anger that challenges a violence
in a world never questioned before;
the timing that starts a movement
for justice never thought important before.
This is the work of the Spirit
and we are filled with praise.

The beauty that smells the perfume of a flower
never known before;
the throat that speaks the names of the silenced
never named before;
the pain that voices the hurt of the past
never acknowledged before.
This is the work of the Spirit
and we are filled with praise.

SEASON AFTER PENTECOST

Trinity Sunday
First Sunday after Pentecost

LECTIONARY READINGS
Isaiah 6:1–8
Psalm 29
Romans 8:12–17
John 3:1–17

One: Come stand before God,
who comes to us as creator, parent, holy and mighty one.
Come stand in the presence of God
and sense God's mystery and creative power
in our world.
Come and proclaim,
"Holy, holy, holy God!"

Two: Come stand before God,
who comes to us in
Jesus – our friend and redeemer.
Come and learn
of God's free gifts
of forgiveness, healing, and grace.
Come and proclaim, "Holy, holy, holy God!"

Three: Come and stand before God,
who comes to us
as Holy Spirit, sanctifier, comforter.
Come and receive

the promise of new, strong hearts and hands
to do God's work in the world.
Come and proclaim, "Holy, holy, holy God!"

* * *

Mighty God, you have created our world,
redeemed it,
and blessed it with your powerful Holy Spirit.
We know that nothing we do
can make us worthy
to receive the gifts you give so freely,
and so we rely on your grace when we fall short in
declaring your glory
or fail to love others as you have loved us.
Call us into ways of living that
reflect the light of your love
to a world that hungers
for your truth and justice.
Cleanse us and make us new.
Hear our words of confession,
and take our guilt away.

* * *

Almighty and ever-present God, you have gifted us with sight and smell and touch and taste and hearing. Through all our senses, you come to us; calling us to know you, and love you, and live for you. Help us hear your call and grant us wisdom to respond with understanding and courage. Amen.

* * *

Creator, Redeemer, and Sustainer,
God of our past, our present, and our future,
no mystery is too strange for you, no task too difficult.
We thank you, God, that though we are weak, you are strong,
and though we are ignorant, you are wise.
You reach out to us with your strong arm and wise spirit –

help us to reach back and grasp what you are so eager to give:
your companionship, your guidance, your grace.
God of all generations, as one age flows into another,
your love binds us to all who came before us
and all who will come after us.
We know, God, that we are all your beloved children,
all precious in your sight, and that you grieve with all who grieve,
and suffer with all who suffer.
We pray that you inspire us with your truth, power and love,
that we may use the talents you've given us to be instruments of your peace,
and work with passion and energy.
For the day that is surely coming when the lion will lie down with the lamb.
We pause now for a moment of silence to lift up to you our personal prayers for ourselves, those whom we love, and the concerns on our hearts…
(*pause for time of silence*).
May we always remember, God, the wideness of your mercy and love.
Grant each one of us the strength, guidance, and inspiration we need
for today's tasks and responsibilities,
and the wisdom to turn over to you our anxieties about tomorrow.
We lift up these prayers, trusting in the fullness of your love and grace. Amen.

* * *

One: Author of life, through your ongoing creativity we marvel at the invitation to go and be likewise; to gently lay hold of the gifts we have been given and to share them open-handedly. For we yearn for a greater creativity in our world with the common good in mind. We long for minds and hearts devoted to peace and good will, not more technologies of war and disunity. Hear the desire of our hearts.

Two: Companion on the journey, as you continually gave of yourself for others and their well-being, may we also give freely. May we stand beside those most in need, offering encouragement and healing. For we yearn for greater compassion in ourselves and in our world. We long for minds and hearts devoted to a common human destiny; not one nation, one religion, or one economy. Hear the desire of our hearts.

Three: Guide us on our way. As you demonstrate the unrehearsed nature of love in its desire to bring renewed life, may we follow with expectation and joy. May we be courageous, even outrageous, because of your call to include and value unconditionally. For we yearn for a vision that we can trust. We long for a life beyond mere patriotism or survival of the strong. Hear the desire of our hearts.

* * *

God of loving kindness,
we bring these gifts as we offer ourselves
in the very real hope
that we may contribute to the peace
and well-being of your world.

* * *

The hands of God uphold you.
The hands of the Saviour enfold you.
The hands of the Spirit surround you.
And the blessing of God;
Trinity of love, peace, and justice,
uphold you for evermore.

Sunday between June 5 and June 11 inclusive (if after Trinity Sunday)

Proper 5 [10]

LECTIONARY READINGS
1 Samuel 8:4–11, (12–15), 16–20, (11:14–15)
Psalm 138
2 Corinthians 4:13—5:1
Mark 3:20–35

We thank you, Creator God, for your vision for justice and wholeness for our world. May we grow in your love, wisdom, and presence so that in the face of injustice and suffering we may become leaders helping to usher in your peace to all creation. Amen.

* * *

One:	Listen! Too many sounds, too many voices, too many people shouting in our ears.
All:	**To whom do we listen?**
One:	We listen to the television pundits, thinking they will tell us what we need to know.
All:	**But do we listen to God?**
One:	We listen to advertisements, thinking they will give what we need.
All:	**But do we listen to God?**
One:	We listen to others' judgments, thinking they will show us the way.
All:	**But do we listen to God?**
One:	Listen! To the One who made us, the One who gives us life, the One who will show us the way. Listen, for God is speaking, here in this time and place.

* * *

God who speaks, we want to hear you. We yearn to listen to you above all the noises of our lives. Guide us in this time of worship to hear your voice. Speak to us in the songs, in the Word, in the laughter of the children, and in the chatting with a new friend. Speak to us, God, your children are listening. Amen.

* * *

God, we can be distracted by the constant pressures in our lives: the accounts we have yet to pay, the better job that we haven't applied for, that bigger house we think we need (*sound maker #1 begins banging a pot, but not loud enough to drown out the speaker*).

God, we can be distracted by instantaneous communication: the messages that are pouring in, the calls that keep coming, the social networks that never shut down (*sound maker #2 starts playing a cell/mobile phone ringtone*).

God, we can be distracted by information: the 24-hour news cycle, libraries available at the click of a mouse, medical information changing every day (*sound maker #3 starts reading an article aloud*).

But God, we seek to focus on you (*sound maker #1 stops and is silent*). We want to communicate with you (*sound maker #2 stops and is silent*). We want to know more about you (*sound maker #3 stops and is silent*).
Forgive us for the times when we allow ourselves to be distracted from living in your way, for the times when we want more than we need, and for desiring the secular instead of your way.

God of the world, you listen to us even when we don't listen to you. Hear our prayer and may we hear the sound of your forgiveness. Amen.

God who listens, and who challenges us to listen, we yearn to listen together to the sounds of truth, peace, injustice, and righteousness in our world. Teach us to listen through the distractions and noises of our world, and to create harmonious sounds as a community. Weave our voices together into a song of justice and bind us together so that we may listen, truly listen, to each other, and sing songs of praise together, that you may joyfully listen to us.

God, when we hear joyous news from a friend in the community, we celebrate together (*sound maker #4 starts playing the introduction to a community song*).

God, when we hear about sickness and disease among your people, we lament together (*sound maker #5 starts playing her or his instrument in harmony with, or to the beat of, the community song*).

God, when we hear about injustice in your creation, we work together (*sound maker #6 also starts playing in harmony with the music*).

Listen and hear the word of God, this day, in this place, and in all the places of the world. Remember that when we neglect to listen to each other, God will still listen to us. Amen.

Sunday between June 12 and June 18 inclusive (if after Trinity Sunday)

Proper 6 [11]

LECTIONARY READINGS
1 Samuel 15:34—16:13
Psalm 20
2 Corinthians 5:6–10, (11–13), 14–17
Mark 4:26–34

God of grace and fresh beginnings, open our eyes and spirits to see the possibilities around and within us. Grant us faith that trusts your working in new ways, through every child fashioned in your image and called to your service. Amen.

* * *

Loving God, teach us to see with your eyes of compassion and wisdom, so that we may understand your will for our world. Help us to discover and hear those who may have been overlooked or ignored, and let us heed each other's voices as we seek your peace and justice in our lives. Amen.

* * *

O God, open the windows of our hearts that we may breathe in deeply of your Spirit.
Enable us to hear words of life we have never heard before,
and see visions of hope we never thought possible, so that we might more fully become the people you have called us to be. Amen.

* * *

Holy One,
whose very presence is creative, effusive love,
we acknowledge in ourselves
an all too careful approach to life and faith.
Free us to live in the creative moment, O God.

We confess the need to be in control
by forcing our will upon others
and demanding changes
that we ourselves would never be able to make.
Free us to live in the creative moment, O God.

May our reason be shaken by astonishment,
our opinions tempered by wonder,
and our well-made plans
undone by new horizons of experience.
Free us to live in the creative moment, O God.

* * *

Gift-giving God, we confess that we do not always know our own worth, that we can forget our capacity for greatness and squander opportunities for righteousness. You offer us gifts for service in your world, and yet we can neglect your gifts, store them away in the closet, shove them under the stairs, and give away to others the gifts you have chosen especially for us. May we have wisdom to know our gifts, courage to open them up, and dedication to use them for your glory. Amen.

* * *

God has created us not for fear or doubt, but for power and love. Rejoice in the giftedness of God's creation, knowing that each and every one of us is created with a special purpose, a special calling, a special gift. Amen.

* * *

One: God, who surprises us with gifts we didn't even know we had, we come to you in thanksgiving. We can see for ourselves the multitude of gifts you have given to this congregation, gifts that may not have been visible to ourselves and others. We give you thanks for the many gifts of our community, especially for the members of our family who speak words of inspiration, who lead us in song, who preach the word:

All:	**God of gifts, we thank you.**
One:	We thank you for the members of our family who care for others, who teach our children, and offer us comfort in times of sadness and grief:
All:	**God of gifts, we thank you.**
One:	For those who are dedicated to the service of the church, who show up early and stay late, those who greet us at the door and keep the budget and plant the flowers:
All:	**God of gifts, we thank you.**
One:	For those members of our family who cannot come to worship, who worship with us from their homes and from many places across the world, those who remind us that our church is not only within these walls, those who worship with us in spirit:
All:	**God of gifts, we thank you.**
One:	For the members of our family who are new to this community, for those who are searching for their gifts to share, and those who seek new ways of being the church:
All:	**God of gifts, we thank you.**
One:	And we thank you for all these gifts we have shared, gifts we have placed before you, and gifts we have not yet seen:
All:	**God of gifts, we thank you.**

* * *

Creator God,
for the miracle of life
silently going on
around and through us
every second of the day,
we give you great thanks.
May we also be wasteful,
flourishing givers of life and love,
and may these presented gifts
reflect that heartfelt desire.

* * *

One:	If anyone is in Christ there is a new creation: everything old has passed away: See, everything has become new! God is opening up new paths before us.
All:	**Let us step forth boldly.**
One:	And may the blessing of God, Creator, Redeemer, and Sustainer, be with us in each new moment, this day and always.
All:	**Amen.**

Sunday between June 19 and June 25 inclusive (if after Trinity Sunday)

Proper 7 [12]

LECTIONARY READINGS
1 Samuel 17:(1a, 4–11, 19–23), 32–49
Psalm 9:9–20
2 Corinthians 6:1–13
Mark 4:35–41

In times of storm and in places of calm: we give thanks, O God, for your presence.
In calls to go and in gifts of peace: we give you thanks, O God, for your word.
May we follow your leading, as we trust your purposes. In Jesus Christ. Amen.

* * *

Loving God, we do not always make your ways our ways.
Help us to respond to the challenges we face with a courage born out of believing that you will provide the wisdom and strength we need. Amen.

* * *

We thank you, mighty God, that the even the least among us can trust in you to be our champion and protector. We pray that you would continue to build our trust in your strength and vision that we may join your pursuit for justice and peace for all. Amen.

* * *

Leader: Come in from the storm.
Come, find rest from the trials that tire you.
Come, find strength to face the powers that frighten you.

All: **We trust in God.**
Even the wind and the waves obey God's voice.

Leader: Come in from the storm!
Come, seek wisdom
to engage the foes who oppress you.
Come, seek courage
to stand with those who struggle with injustice.
All: **We trust in God.**
God is our rock and our strength in times of trouble.

Leader: Come in from the storm!
Come, proclaim that with God, nothing is hopeless.
Come, proclaim that God will show a better way.
All: **We trust in God.**
We rejoice that God is our strength and salvation.

* * *

One: Power is…
All: **the ability to enact change.**
One: Power wants…
All: **to be a force for liberation.**
One: Power gives…
All: **a voice to the voiceless.**
One: Power needs…
All: **to be examined, challenged, and critiqued.**
One: Power comes…
All: **from a powerful God.**
One: Let us come together in the power of worship.

* * *

Great God of heaven and earth,
we are often aware of your power.
It comes to us in a booming voice in the thunder
and in majestic views of mountain and ocean,
and times of thunder and blizzard.

Yet your power is also seen in the colours of a ladybug and a child's cry.
In all these things and much, much more,
we are reminded of your awesome greatness.
In this time of worship may we appreciate and celebrate your power,
and may we always seek ways to use it for peace and goodness. Amen.

* * *

All: **God of mercy, you are the origin of all that is and the centre of power in all that is. Too often we consider ourselves to be more powerful than we are. We enjoy control and seek dominance; we oppress those with less power than ourselves, and deny the innate human power that you have created in us. Forgive our vain attempts to manipulate and our propensity to diminish ourselves. Help us to remember all those whose voices are marginalized by unjust systems that we have created, and give us powerful vision to overcome the obstacles that impede your will. We pray in Christ's name. Amen.**

* * *

We are so often given over to fear, O God.
Like the disciples we huddle together,
swamped in spirit by the waves of life
in their many different forms.
For it is not as though there
is nothing to be afraid of.
And we need not pretend that
faith puts an end to all doubt.
It is simply that in those difficult
and very human moments
we do not reach out to you.
We do not seek
the reassurance and calm
that you are so willing to give.
Hear then our cry for healing;
hear in our hearts our longing for calming peace.

* * *

As one who journeys with us in life,
never above or beyond us,
we come to God with our prayers:
Hopes for change, cries for meaning,
and concerns for new directions forward.

In the midst of life's great
and many challenges
we cry out to you, O God.
For sometimes the weight of the world's problems
seem overwhelming and we become paralyzed
with the sense that nothing we do
really makes a difference.
Hear our cry and be our healing.

For those who have little hope or joy in life
and those bound by fear and dread, we pray.
Through human warmth and kindness,
courage and persistence,
may there be a crossing over to new ways of being.
Hear our cry and be our healing.

And for a vision that will draw us closer to you
and your ways in the world, we pray.
Strengthen us to seek new ways of being your people,
daring to follow and to imaginatively create
community in the name of Christ.
May our thinking be renewed and our souls enlarged.
Hear our cry and be our healing.

* * *

Go in the peace of God,
which passes all understanding,
daring to care,
daring to share,
and daring to love.
And may the grace of Christ,
the love of God,
and the friendship of the Holy Spirit
go with you, now and always.
Amen!

* * *

One: O God,
you love all you have created
and call us to be your agents
of care and justice.
Hear our prayer for those who struggle.
For all who have no land or home,
All: **be their strength, and give us courage to stand with them.**
One: For all who are hungry,
All: **be their strength, and give us courage to stand with them.**
One: For all who labour in unsafe places, earning unfair wages,
All: **be their strength, and give us courage to stand with them.**
One: For all who seek asylum from prejudice and oppression,
All: **be their strength, and give us courage to stand with them.**
One: God, we place in your strong hands
all the people for whom we pray. Give us all
your strength and courage.
Hear our prayer.
All: Amen.

* * *

One: Believe in the power that God has given to each one of us.
All: **We will go, believing.**
One: Believe that God gives us courage to do great things.
All: **We will go, believing.**
One: Believe that God turns small things into great things.
All: **We will go, believing.**
One: Believe that God chooses ordinary people to do extraordinary things.
All: **We will go, believing.**
One: Believe that God cares for those who are poor and in need.
All: **We will go, believing.**
One: Believe that God can help us find a new way to accomplish what seems to be impossible.
All: **We will go, believing.**
Amen.

Sunday between June 26 and July 2 inclusive

Proper 8 [13]

LECTIONARY READINGS
2 Samuel 1:1, 17–27
Psalm 130
2 Corinthians 8:7–15
Mark 5:21–43

Out of the depths we cry to you, O God. And into the depths you accompany us. You hear, even before we find words. You grieve, even as we feel the pain. You love, long before we give voice to trust. So we wait and hope in your presence. Amen.

* * *

Our souls wait for God, more than those who watch for the morning. More than those who watch for the morning our souls wait. With hope in our hearts we watch and wait (*Psalm 130:5, paraphrased*).

* * *

God of all our longings,
you are the fire that kindles our hearts
with hope and possibility.
You fill us with desire for life,
and you hear our voices whether we shout for joy
or cry out with sorrow.
We trust in you and give thanks for your presence
in all the stages of our life.
Help us to be open to the movement
of your Holy Spirit in our world. Amen.

* * *

One:	In the midst of life's chaos,
Two:	at the heart of our discontent,
Three:	within the fragments of human brokenness,
All:	**lives the healing presence of God.**

One:	Beyond our fears and misgivings,
Two:	before the excuses and doubting,
Three:	at home within the honest and vulnerable,
All:	**lives the healing power of God.**

One:	Come, let us not pretend we do not know these places.
Two:	Let us not avoid what is most real.
Three:	For in the facing and the accepting,
All:	**lives the healing embrace of God.**

* * *

Guide people through a movement from spiritual resistance toward an open and healing acceptance. Invite people to assume a posture of resistance such as closed eyes clenched fists, crossed arms, and hunched shoulders. When the words, "Heal us..." are spoken, invite people to assume an open posture such as open eyes, loosened grip, unfolded arms, and slow, deep breaths. Demonstrate how they are to bring their hands out to the side, opening them upwards and leaving them raised until the end of the prayer. Use the questions as moments for natural pause. These pauses are helpful to the imagination.

I will not yield so easily.
I will not hand over everything.
This is my life and it is for me to control.

Yet, why then of late, O God,
does it seem that very little is working?
Why is my confidence left shaken
and I'm left feeling anything but strong?
In fact, I feel fragile and uncertain
in ways I have felt before.

Might it be that I'm running on empty?
That at the end of my own resources
is the beginning of your own?
That my own desire and ability to love
needs to be filled with the gift of love itself?

Heal us, O God.
(Give people time to take on a new posture.)
Heal us, O God, of the need to avoid
the hidden places.
Open our hearts and minds
to a grace and goodness
that finds us exactly where we are,
and which touches us deeply,
lifting us up to new and creative lives.

* * *

Broken bodies, shamed peoples,
and ravaged eco-systems;
it's not the world of your making, O God,
but it is the world in which we live
and daily seek to make a positive difference.
In the silence and led by your Spirit,
we yearn for healing,
we wait for your saving Presence. *(silence)*

Deceit of the powerful, complicity of the masses
and wars that most injure the innocent;
it's certainly not your Reign, O God,
but it is the world in which we live
and daily seek to make a positive difference.
In the silence and led by your Spirit,
we yearn for healing,
we wait for your saving Presence. *(silence)*

Exclusive religions, "truths" set in stone,
and leaders beyond accountability;
it's not what Jesus hoped and prayed for,
but it is the world in which we live
and daily seek to make a positive difference.
In the silence and led by your Spirit,
we yearn for healing,
we wait for your saving Presence. *(silence)*

Sunday between July 3 and July 9 inclusive

Proper 9 [14]

LECTIONARY READINGS
2 Samuel 5:1–5, 9–10
Psalm 48
2 Corinthians 12:2–10
Mark 6:1–13

Merciful God, when we experience moments of weakness and rejection in your name, help us recall not only your power and might but your compassion for your people. Grant us the courage and the faith to continue our fight against suffering, injustice, and hatred in our world. Amen.

* * *

We come together in this place
where the ordinary becomes sanctified
and the familiar is made new.
Make us mindful, O Prophetic One,
of your call on our lives
and of the Spirit's power.
Fill us with holy imagination and vision
as we gather up the courage
to live as your people in this world.

* * *

One leader, portraying Jesus, stands in the centre of the worship space. On either side of him or her, line up ten people, single file. These will be Side 1 and Side 2. One by one, each of the people on Side 1 will step forward and read the prayer. After each prayer the person portraying Jesus will gesture for the next person on Side 2 to step forward and read their prayer. The two people will then link arms and walk down the centre of the worship space and back to their seats (preferably sitting together for the remainder of the service). The idea for this prayer is to demonstration that we are called to partner with others to bring acceptance to the rejected in our midst.

Side 1

One: We pray for the isolated.
Two: We pray for the immigrant.
Three: We pray for those who are persecuted because of their sexual identity.
Four: We pray for victims of war and conflict.
Five: We pray for people struggling with addiction.
Six: We pray for the doubters.
Seven: We pray for the disabled and the differently-abled.
Eight: We pray for those who suffer alone and in silence.
Nine: We pray for our enemies.
Ten: We pray for
(insert a particular need in your community).

Side 2

One: Give us community.
Two: Give us safe passage.
Three: Give us justice.

Four: Give us peace.

Five: Give us strength.

Six: Give us wisdom.
Seven: Give us understanding.

Eight: Give us comfort.

Nine: Give us love.
Ten: Give us
(insert the request such as grace, forgiveness, strength).

* * *

Invite the congregation to hold hands with the people on either side of them, as a symbol of acceptance and inclusion.

Go out into God's world with a commitment to make others feel loved and welcomed. And know that you yourselves are loved and welcomed by God, who has called you by name and knows you by heart. Amen.

✷ ✷ ✷

God has spoken,
"I am sending you in love –
imagine the possibilities.
My love is all you need.
Colour the world with it,
spread it throughout your speaking,
honour it within your living.
Go now, for God has called you,
Christ has sent you,
and Spirit has empowered you."

Sunday between July 10 and July 16 inclusive

Proper 10 [15]

LECTIONARY READINGS
2 Samuel 6:1–5, 12b–19
Psalm 24
Ephesians 1:3–14
Mark 6:14–29

Open our hearts, O God, so that we might perceive your presence and respond in joy. Make us bold to praise you in solitude and in community – singing, dancing, and playing to tell of your glory. Amen.

* * *

All:	**God has forgiven us.**
One:	For the times when we have embraced poor relationships, God has shown us mercy.
All:	**God has forgiven us.**
One:	For the sins we have committed against our families in the past, God has shown us mercy.
All:	**God has forgiven us.**
One:	For our short-sightedness and bigotry against others, God has shown us mercy.
All:	**God has forgiven us.**
One:	For the times when we have forgotten the struggles of the world, God has shown us mercy.
All:	**God has forgiven us.**
One:	For the times when Christianity was a burden and not a blessing to the world, God has shown us mercy.
All:	**God has forgiven us.**

One: There is much to be done – justice to be found, forgiveness to be earned, wrongs to be righted. But God has adopted us all of many faiths into one big family of faith, and because of God's unending love, undeserved by us, we are forgiven.
All: **Thanks be to God. Amen.**

* * *

O God, your presence is made known to us
in this gathered community of faith,
in the doing of justice and evidence of peace,
in the face of a stranger and the story of a friend.
May we recognize the sacred at all times and places
and be inspired with your joy.
Give us the courage and freedom
to express this joy in every way and with all that we are.

* * *

One: Embracing God, you have adopted us into your family and freely given to us the life-giving salvation of Jesus Christ. Yet we have neglected our own families, in our homes and throughout the world.
For the times when we have neglected our own families, preferring selfish pursuits, God have mercy.
All: **God, forgive us.**
One: For the members of our family who have hurt and wronged us, for the times when we have endured life-destroying language and embraced life-damaging relationships, God have mercy.
All: **God, forgive us.**
One: For the sins of the past, for the times when we have harboured ill will against our families and for the times when we have wronged them, God have mercy.
All: **God, forgive us.**
One: For the ways that our world limits what a family can be,

	and for the times we have preferred the comfort of tradition rather than the complexity of love, God have mercy.
All:	**God, forgive us.**
One:	For the struggling families of our world, families that are parented by children who have no other option, families that struggle for the basic necessities of life, families that are separated by our immigration policies, God have mercy.
All:	**God, forgive us.**
One:	For the ways that our Christian tradition has usurped the traditions of other communities of faith, limiting our family to those who profess the same things that we profess, and for the ways that we interpret God's word so that it blesses only us, God have mercy.
All:	**God, forgive us.**

* * *

O God, breath of our souls, you are the heartbeat of our delight and longing. We give you thanks for all the moments of our lives that are filled with the joy of being your creatures on this amazing planet. Thank you for the languages of music and rhythm that cross all boundaries. Thank you for all the signs and symbols of your presence with us. Help us to be the song you sing and the movement you dance so that with your people throughout the whole earth, we might enjoy the glorious life that you lavish upon your beloved world. Amen.

***

During this prayer, allow for times of silent prayer and, building on the theme of David's dance before God, you might fill the silence with body prayer of interpretive dance. Ask the dancer(s) to keep prayerful expressions brief (no longer than one minute). At the conclusion of each prayer, offer the following response.

Leader: O God, hear our prayer.
All: **Help us to move with you in your dance
of healing and justice.**
One: Fount of all life, dancing in bliss,
All: **breaking down walls, making new spaces,**
One: burning up evil, creating afresh,
All: **calling your people, follow in faith.**
One: Living with Jesus, power in his name,
All: **healing the broken, restoring those who are wounded.**

* * *

Distribute strips of colourful cloth or streamers. After the words of sending are given, invite people to move in a celebrative way with their cloth/streamers as they exit. A song such as the chorus of "Lord of the Dance" would provide fitting procession music.

Let us move forward into our world with delight,
knowing that we are part of the great divine dance of life.
May the blessing of God
the dancer and the dance,
move with us and within us
this day and always.

Sunday between July 17 and July 23 inclusive

Proper 11 [16]

LECTIONARY READINGS
2 Samuel 7:1–14a
Psalm 89:20–37
Ephesians 2:11–22
Mark 6:30–34, 53–56

God, we pray for the gift of place – a space where we may experience your presence, where we may attend to the needs of others and ourselves, where we may rest, and where we may serve. For in such a place do we find life and hope, now and always. Amen.

* * *

O God, in you we live and move and have our being.
With you we are always at home.
Help us, through Christ,
to know and experience this reality
with every cell in our bodies,
so that with Christ and in Christ
we might love you and worship you
with all our hearts. Amen.

* * *

This prayer was written by a group of young people in response to a Homelessness Awareness Weekend at their church. You may wish to adapt it to situations in your community.

One: Those who are homeless can be seen in doorways,
in bus stations, in parks, and on the roadside. They
can be found in abandoned buildings, in shelters,

	and in parked cars. In the hustle and bustle of our lives we walk by them, for they are invisible to us.
All:	**O God, help us slow down our fast-paced lives and give us the strength to open our eyes to those who are homeless.**
One:	They are the men, women, and children who due to unfortunate circumstances are left without a place to live and food to nourish them.
All:	**O God, you call us to help them, as best we are able.**
One:	They have stories rich in both joy and sadness to tell. They seem voiceless, because we are too involved in our own lives to take time to listen.
All:	**O God, please help us to find the courage to stop and listen to the stories of your people.**
One:	Often they are lonesome, with very few people willing to care for them or to provide them with the warmth they deserve.
All:	**O God, help us to open our hearts to accept your people whom society has abandoned.**
One:	They are your children. They are similar to us. They too have hopes, dreams, desires, and aspirations.
All:	**O God, help us open our minds so we may recognize all on the earth as your people.**
One:	These are your people filled with your love and goodness – although often overlooked.
All:	**O God, open our minds to allow us to see the beauty in all of your people.**
One:	They frighten us because we do not know their stories. They frighten us because deep down we know that we can easily become one of them.
All:	**O God, forgive us for our fears and help us to remember that your light shines through them just as brightly as it shines through any of your children. Amen.**

* * *

Let us leave this place
knowing that wherever we go,
God is there, at home in the whole creation.
May the blessing of God –
creator, redeemer, and sustainer –
be with us in all the places of our lives,
this day and always. Amen.

Sunday between July 24 and July 30 inclusive

Proper 12 [17]

LECTIONARY READINGS
2 Samuel 11:1–15
Psalm 14
Ephesians 3:14–21
John 6:1–21

Bring a piece of dried crust on a plate, a small loaf of bread in a basket, and a pita on a plate. Arrange to have three people read the three stanzas of prayer as they perform the instructed movements.

One: O God, sometimes we feel
like dry crumbs on a cold plate
(crumble a piece of crust onto a plate).
Lackluster living,
depleted energy,
meaningless existence
in a cold, uncaring world *(pause).*

Two: Sometimes we feel like a loaf of bread
broken and disregarded
(tear a small loaf in half and place in basket).
Torn in too many directions,
divided allegiances,
worn thin *(pause).*

Three: Sometimes we feel
like stale, unleavened bread
(break a pita in half).
Dispirited,
dried up,
wondering how to carry on *(pause).*

All: **Gather us into the breadbasket
of your love, O God.
Renew our dried up spirits.
Heal our brokenness.
Lift us with the friendship of this community.
Shape us into your people once again.**

✶ ✶ ✶

One: Loving God,
in the privilege of prayer we come,
speaking what is in our hearts for others.
All: **May we be signs of God's presence.**
One: We pray your blessing
on every commitment to feed hungry people,
so that both the one who gives
and the one who receives are honoured.
All: **May we be signs of God's presence.**
One: We pray for people
burdened by fears of scarcity,
and for those whose anxiety
is not based in their need.
All: **May we be signs of God's presence.**
One: We pray for people
who are afraid to embrace your abundance
and for those who are learning
to trust and believe
in your abundant provision for their lives.
All: **May we be signs of God's presence.**
One: We pray for workers
in health care and public education
where the needs are great and the resources are
dwindling.
All: **May we be signs of God's presence.**
One: We pray for students
and all those needing health care,
asking wisdom for those whose decisions affect their lives.
All: **May we be signs of God's presence.**

One: We pray for countries and relationships
mired in conflict
and ask that your peace break into their lives
with power and freedom.
All: **May we be signs of God's presence.**
One: We pray that this congregation
will be free from fear,
cooperating with your abundance
in all that we are together.
All: **May we be signs of God's presence.**
One: May we receive with joy
the full measure of our days
always knowing that twelve baskets
are not enough
to measure the abundance of your love
or the bounty of your grace
at work in us and all around us.
That the world may be filled with the fullness of God!
All: **May we be signs of God's presence. Amen.**

* * *

God of overflowing grace,
we admit those times when we are timid to offer
what we have,
when we feel our gifts may be too small
to make a difference,
or when we belittle the offerings of others.
Forgive us when we lack faith.
There are times, too, when we are afraid to step forward,
when we do not encourage others,
when we do not dare, or risk, or trust.
Forgive us when we lack faith.
And there are times when we believe we know
all that can be known,
and will not open ourselves
to the wondrous possibilities of the love and grace
you make known to us in Christ Jesus.
Forgive us when we lack faith. Amen.

* * *

Sunday between July 31 and August 6 inclusive

Proper 13 [18]

LECTIONARY READINGS
2 Samuel 11:26—12:13a
Psalm 51:1-12
Ephesians 4:1-16
John 6:24-35

Giver of manna, feed our deepest hungers. Break the bread that nourishes relationship.
Bread the bread that nourishes life in your presence.
We seek you, for you are our life. Amen.

* * *

You call us to gather together as Christ's Body,
loving God, and you send your Spirit to unite us as one.
Cleanse our hearts. Open our minds.
Feed us with your word. Make us new.
In Jesus' name we pray. Amen.

* * *

One:	In humility and trust,
	we confess our shortcomings to you.
Two:	Create in us clean hearts, O God,
All:	**and put a new and right spirit within us.**
One:	In our freedom to make choices in life,
	we have not always chosen wisely
	for ourselves or for others.
Two:	Create in us clean hearts, O God,
All:	**and put a new and right spirit within us.**
One:	As stewards of your creation,
	our dominion has often been cruel.
	We have not always walked lightly on this earth
	or protected it.

Two:	Create in us clean hearts, O God,
All:	**and put a new and right spirit within us.**
One:	Wonderfully made in your image, we sometimes doubt our own holiness.
Two:	Create in us clean hearts, O God,
All:	**and put a new and right spirit within us.**
One:	As a community filled with many gifts, we have not always seen those gifts in others or called them forth for the good of all.
Two:	Create in us clean hearts, O God,
All:	**and put a new and right spirit within us.**
One:	In our common prayer restore to us the joy of your salvation and sustain in us a willing spirit. Ready our hands, our hearts, and our minds to freely give and receive the goodness of new life with you.
Two:	Create in us clean hearts, O God,
All:	**and put a new and right spirit within us.**

* * *

Sisters and brothers,
let the past be the past.
The present is grace.
The future is hope.
This is God's way of forgiveness
for you and for all creation.
Thanks be to God. Amen.

* * *

God, we pray for the apostles, for those who go out into your world and spread the gospel according to their gifts. We pray for missionaries and servants, for those who find that they can share their faith at work or with their family, even when it is difficult.

God, we pray for the prophets, for the writers, for the artists, for the poets, for those who shout against the crowds, speak truth to power, and challenge each of us to new thinking.

God, we pray for the evangelists, for those whose service is never done, for those who visit the hospital and preach good news to the sick, who feed the hungry, clothe the naked, and give hope to the hopeless.

God, we pray for the pastors, for the visible leaders of our community who lead us and follow us according to your grace. We pray that they might use their talents to build up the whole of our community, and that they might have the strength and wisdom to represent our church and the Christian faith to others in our community. Bless these leaders into the life of the Body of Christ.

And God, we pray for the teachers, for those who are tender and patient and careful, who explain things to us in ways we understand, who help to shape us into the people you have called us to be.

For all these people, and all the ways you have called us into your service, we offer praise and thanks to you. Amen.

* * *

Divide the congregation into two groups.

All:	**We are all gifts to each other – one body in Christ.**
Group 1:	Each one has a calling from God.
Group 2:	Each one has grace from Christ.
All:	**We are all gifts to each other – one body in Christ.**
Group 1:	Christ joins and knits us together.
Group 2:	Our gifts build up the whole body.
All:	**We are all gifts to each other – one body in Christ.**

* * *

Leader: Take with you the blessing of your calling,
   the grace Christ has given you,
   and the certainty that no one else
   can take your place among God's people.
   You are a gift to the Body of Christ,
   Now be a gift to God's world.
All: **Thanks be to God!**

* * *

Gathered by God's hopeful love
around a table of welcome;
we affirm the goodness of life
and celebrate its Author's presence.
(Set the table with colourful cloth and a candle.)

Receivers of living bread
that keeps on being broken for all;
we affirm the goodness of life
and pledge ourselves to its sharing.
(Place bread and wine on the table.)

Bearers of a compassionate spirit
who always leads us toward others;
we affirm the goodness of life
and open our hearts to its healing ways.
(Place a pitcher of water and flowers on the table.)

* * *

Giver of life, inspired by your creative love;
may we help create a new world with you.
Bread of life, nourished by your healing love;
may we help create a new world with you.
Spirit of life, filled with your compassionate love;
may we help create a new world with you.

* * *

Sunday between August 7 and August 13 inclusive

Proper 14 [19]

LECTIONARY READINGS
2 Samuel 18:5–9, 15, 31–33
Psalm 130
Ephesians 4:25—5:2
John 6:35, 41–51

We accept the love of Christ,
which is for us, and for all people.
We desire to be changed by this love
that we might bless the world
and each other
with kindness,
tender-heartedness,
and forgiveness.
Let Christ's love grow to rule our lives in everything. Amen.

* * *

We give thanks to you, God,
for our lives, which you have blessed.
You lead us through days when the shadow of death overtakes us,
and keep our hearts tender in the midst of loss and disappointment.
We pray for people whose hearts are breaking,
and for people who are afraid to love and be loved.
Alleluia! Love is a gift from God.

We give thanks to you, God,
for giving us a ministry of reconciliation in this world.
We give you thanks for Jesus Christ, who is our peace.
We pray for broken relationships in families and among friends.
We pray for peace within congregations and between countries
and cultures.

May all be reconciled through your peace.
Alleluia! Love is a gift from God.

We give you thanks, O God,
for the gift of being made one of your people,
and being given a spiritual home in the Body of Christ.
We pray for our congregation and its leaders.
Nurture in each of us a seasoned faith and give birth to a lively faith in our midst.
Alleluia! Love is a gift from God.

We give thanks to you, O God,
for trusting us to be stewards of your word,
and witnesses to your works of forgiveness, healing, and freedom.
We give thanks for the hope you place among us in the promises of your word.
We pray that we will trust you in return, believing in your transforming power, proclaiming it with confidence, and opening ourselves to it even as we welcome others to its hope.
Alleluia! Love is a gift from God.

We give thanks to you, O God,
that this morning we have opened our eyes to a new day and the privilege of life.
We pray for people who have come to fear a new day, for those who are depressed,
and for those who have lost the joy of seeing what is good and wondrous in this world.
Alleluia! Love is a gift from God.

* * *

Invite people to place their hands near their hearts during the words of the leader, and then to open them outward, then lift them upward during their responses.

Leader: Loving God, grant us wisdom and strength to carry your love into our world.
All: Open our hearts to care, O God, and strengthen our hands to help.
Leader: Grant your healing touch to those who are sick, and to those who are waiting for medical treatment and test results.
All: Open our hearts to care, O God, and strengthen our hands to help.
Leader: Grant your peace to people living with mental illness and to those who are in emotional distress.
All: Open our hearts to care, O God, and strengthen our hands to help.
Leader: Grant your protection to those who live in danger and to those who are not able to care for themselves.
All: Open our hearts to care, O God, and strengthen our hands to help.
Leader: Grant your guidance to people of all ages who seek to know you and create communities that are guided by your love.
All: Open our hearts to care, O God, and strengthen our hands to help.

* * *

Grant me the grace, O God,
to know what I should know,
to love what I should love,
to praise what pleases you, and
to cherish everything
that is precious to you.
Keep me from judging simply
by what my eyes see, or my ears hear;
help me to know the difference
between appearance and spiritual reality.
Above all, may I have the grace
always to seek your joy.
Amen.

Thomas à Kempis

* * *

Sunday between August 14 and August 20 inclusive

Proper 15 [20]

LECTIONARY READINGS
1 Kings 2:10–12, 3:3–14
Psalm 111
Ephesians 5:15–20
John 6:51–58

Introduce a breathing prayer. Recall that one name for God in the Hebrew Scriptures is "YHWH," spelled without vowels because no vowels were used in ancient Hebrew. While praying, breathe in while sighing "YH" and breathe out while sighing "WH." Invite people to breathe and sigh these syllables as they silently offer their gathering prayer or offer confession to God. Do not be hasty in concluding this prayerful opening.

Leader: God always hears our prayers.
All: **Amen. Amen. Amen. Let it be so!**

* * *

O God, holy wisdom, we open the windows of our hearts to you
and the life you give.
Help us to breathe in deeply of your Spirit.
Feed us with your bread of life;
inspire us with your awesome presence
so that we might more fully become the people you have called
us to be. Amen.

* * *

Hallelujah! With all my heart I praise you, Holy One,
in the congregation of truthful people.
    How great are your works,
pondered by all who delight in them.
Majesty and splendour clothe them,
always faithful and just.
    Your wondrous deeds have won renown;
you are so gracious and merciful.
Food you give to those who revere you.
    Always you remember your covenant.
The power of your works
you show to your people,
by giving them the heritage of nations.
    Your handiwork is true and just;
all your precepts worthy of trust,
enduring forever,
performed in faithfulness and truth.
    You sent redemption to your people,
ordained your convenant for all time;
holy and revered is your name.
The beginning of wisdom
is reverence for you, Holy One;
sound insight comes to all who follow it.
    Your praise continues forever!
With all our hearts we praise you, O Holy One.

* * *

Divide into two groups. Group one reads from column 1, group 2 from column 2. Group one begins with one person saying, "We pray for the unwise" and group 2 responds with one person saying, "We want to act wisely..." Continue in this way, alternating "One" and "All" for the rest of the prayer.

One:	We pray for the unwise.	**One:**	We want to act wisely; grant us wisdom.
All:	**We pray for those we love.**	**All:**	**We pray for those we have never met.**
One:	We pray for those who are lonely.	**One:**	We pray for those who are sad.
All:	**We pray for victims of war.**	**All:**	**We will work for peace.**
One:	We pray for those struggling with addiction.	**One:**	We pray for patience and compassion.
All:	**We pray for those without hope.**	**All:**	**Grant us tangible hope to share with all.**
One:	We pray for all who are weary.	**One:**	May their burdens be shared.
All:	**We pray for our enemies.**	**All:**	**Help us to love as you love us.**
One:	We pray for those who have been silenced.	**One:**	Enable us to share their song with other.
All:	**We pray for the hungry.**	**All:**	**May all the world share the food we have.**
One:	Help us to live carefully.	**One:**	Help us to live wisely.
All:	**Help us to rejoice in all things.**	**All:**	**Help us to be grateful in all things.**
One:	In the name of your child,	**One:**	Our wise teacher, we pray,
All:	**Amen.**	**All:**	**Amen.**

* * *

When Solomon became king of Israel,
he asked God to gift him with wisdom –
the ability to know and the will to do God's justice.
Like Solomon, we are called
to care for our homeland: the earth.

We are not afraid of this awesome responsibility
for God gifts us with wisdom
to know and do what is right and just.
Let us live in the wisdom of God
and be faithful in all that is entrusted to us.

* * *

People of God, make the most of these times!
Be filled with the Spirit.
Seek wisdom and give thanks to God always.

Sunday between August 21 and August 27 inclusive

Proper 16 [21]

LECTIONARY READINGS
1 Kings 8:(1, 6, 10–11), 22–30, 41–43
Psalm 84
Ephesians 6:10–20
John 6:56–69

God of Power, God of Peace, you equip us to face the existential,
political, and spiritual challenges of this and every era.
May we be mindful of your protection, and help us share your word
in ways that promote love, grace, and justice.
In Jesus' name. Amen.

* * *

Give us your heart, O God,
as we pray for the world you so deeply love.
We pray for areas of conflict and war
especially where people seek reconciliation.
Help us to put on your strength, O God.
We pray for protection against any power that would hurt us
or others.
Help us to put on your strength, O God.
We pray for protection against any power that would hurt us
or others.
Help us to put on your strength, O God.
We pray for people burdened with grief or illness.
Help them to rest in the strength of this community which is
supporting them.
Help us to put on your strength, O God.
We pray for children who are asked to grow up too soon.
Give them wisdom and confidence beyond their years.

Help us to put on your strength, O God.
Enfold our prayers, O God, into your sacred purposes.
We ask this in your strong name.
Help us to put on your strength, O God.

* * *

We are glad to gather here in this place, and to call it your house. Yet we are mindful of times when we tend to think that this is the only place you dwell. When we want to leave you here on Sunday mornings,
Gracious God, forgive us.
When we tend to think that you prefer this house to others in our community or around the world,
Gracious God, forgive us.
When we exclude others with our theology, language, traditions, and practices.
Gracious God, forgive us.
When our structures keep others out,
Gracious God, forgive us.
When we fail to make your house a place where the good news is proclaimed, justice is practiced, and healing is offered to all,
Gracious God, forgive us. Amen.

* * *

Dear friends in Christ,
God's love is greater than all our lack of caring.
God's forgiveness is bigger and wider than any hurt or
harm we can ever receive or give.
So open the windows of your hearts and hear the good news.
We are loved.
We are forgiven.
We live in the grace of God. Amen.

* * *

Sunday between August 28 and September 3 inclusive

Proper 17 [22]

LECTIONARY READINGS
Song of Solomon 2:8–13
Psalm 45:1–2, 6–9
James 1:17–27
Mark 7:1–8, 14–15, 21–23

O God, giver of life,
we turn away from what we understand about you and how you would have us live in the world.
We hear your word and even understand it but then we don't put our whole heart into living by it.
Help us risk living as if your word were implanted in us, impossible to deny or suppress.
Amen.

* * *

One:	I am the circling hawk
	dancing with joy for life.
All:	**God, you invite us to join in the dance!**
One:	I am the faithful soil
	nourishing each life I touch.
All:	**You invite us to join in the caring.**
One:	I am the swift stream
	singing my thanks for life.
All:	**You invite us to join in the song.**
One:	I am the blazing star
	bringing wonder to life.
All:	**You invite us to join in the wonder.**
One:	I am the voice of creation
	praising the God who shapes life:
All:	**You invite us to join in the praise.**

* * *

Generous giver of life,
we pause from our hurrying,
we rest from our scheduling,
and we hold still our anxious minds.
For in your calming presence,
and open to your Spirit,
we seek another way of being,
another way of doing.
May we simply be people
who in our stumbling humanity,
mirror your love and goodness
with joy, purpose, and passion.

* * *

*Read and enact this simple poem. Teach people to say the **bolded response** each time. Say the non-bolded lines and invite people to mimic the actions. Repeat more than once so all get comfortable. Ask what it felt like to use both words and movements about love.*

As people of heart
(hands gently crossed over the heart),
and lovers of life
(hands extended out, palms upward);
we are the people of God,
we are a people of love!

As people who think
(hands gently touching the head),
and givers of peace
(a handshake or embrace where appropriate);
we are the people of God,
we are a people of love!

As people who care
(one hand extended to another),
and healers of hurt
(two hands lifting up another);
we are the people of God,
we are a people of love!

* * *

When we say one thing and do another,
O God, forgive us.
When we know the truth, but do not act on it,
O God, forgive us.
When we fail to notice the overwhelming love you have for all your creation, and all your people,
O God, forgive us.
When we are quick to speak and slow to listen, rather than the other way around,
O God, forgive us.

* * *

Father and Mother of lights,
with whom there is no shadow,
we pray yet again for the world of your making:
We pray with an active hope. We pray in love.
For those born in hopelessness
without parental love
or the provision of basic human needs:
We pray with an active hope. We pray in love.
For those raised in poverty
often unprotected from disease,
or those unable to afford basic health care:
We pray with an active hope. We pray in love.
For those scarred by wars
and consumed by hatred enduring and deep:
We pray with an active hope. We pray in love.
And for those in this place

yearning for healing
or in need of simple understanding and care:
We pray with an active hope. We pray in love.
Mother and Father of lights,
with whom there is no shadow,
hear these and other prayers of the heart.
For you are the source of our hope
and you are the wellspring of our love.
Use us in the remaking of your world.
We pray with an active hope. We pray in love. Amen.

* * *

Invite people to break up into groups of three or four. Have each group form a circle. Have them turn and say to one another, "You are God's beloved, be love for the world." Conclude with a Celtic blessing as the whole community links arms or hands.

On our hearts and on our house
the blessing of God.
In our comings and goings
the peace of God.
At our end and new beginnings
**the arms of God to welcome us
and bring us all home. Amen!**

Sunday between September 4 and September 10 inclusive

Proper 18 [23]

LECTIONARY READINGS
Proverbs 22:1–2, 8–9, 22–23
Psalm 125
James 2:1–10, (11–13), 14–17
Mark 7:24–37

Hear us when we call to you, O God.
For if we cannot turn to you, where can hope be found?
Sharpen us to hear when you call,
especially in the voice of a vulnerable one.
For if others cannot turn to us,
where will faith be found and lived?
Amen.

* * *

Valued without distinction
and called without favour;
we gather in the love of God.
Invited to places of deep change
and entrusted with lives of grace;
we gather in the compassion of Christ.
Encouraged to be authentic
and inspired to make a difference;
we gather in the power of the Spirit.

* * *

God of surprise and awe,
you who can turn our many
hatreds and fears around;
come to us in the time of worship.

**Challenge our sure perspectives
and unsettle our fixed opinions.**
Above all, instill in us
a vision for a new world
and a re-creative way
of living wholeheartedly within it.

* * *

So often, O God, we know the theory,
so often we mouth (and sing) words
of inclusion, compassion, and "justice for all."
Yet the reality remains –
our confession rings true –
**it is a truly difficult thing
to love our neighbours
as they really are;
to feel as they may feel,
and to be as they may be** *(pause)*.

We pray, then, for hearts
open to gradual, yet genuine change.
**May the encounters we seek
and the trust we help create,
bring us to more hopeful understandings
about ourselves and
the world of your making** *(pause)*.

May there be peace in our restlessness;
may there be peace in our time, O God.

* * *

Invite the congregation to learn the response Ephphatha, (pronounced ef-FATH-ah). Invite them to lift up their heads and hands as they speak the response, and to lower them during each petition.

Leader:	In this world many cry for justice, mercy, and healing. Open our hearts to hear their cries. Jesus, speak your word of power and let it be so in our lives.
All:	**Ephphatha.**
Leader:	We bring before you the cries of parents – birth parents, adoptive parents, step-parents, foster parents, and godparents – who seek healing and wholeness for their children. Give us wisdom and courage to reach across boundaries to answer their pleas. Jesus, speak your word of power and let it be so in our lives.
All:	**Ephphatha.**
Leader:	We lift up before you the needs of all who live with illness. Grant us compassion and patience to extend our hands in healing. Jesus, speak your word of power and let it be so in our lives.
All:	**Ephphatha.**
Leader:	We name before you all those who are separated by distance or estrangement. Open our eyes to the boundaries that we have created and give us the strength to cross them with courage. Jesus, speak your word of power and let it be so in our lives.
All:	**Ephphatha.**
Leader:	We cry out for the needs of those whom we hold in our hearts this day. *(Observe a moment of silence. Invite people to call out the names of those for whom they seek prayer.)* Jesus, speak your word of power and let it be so in our lives.
All:	**Ephphatha.**
Leader:	Guide our steps, God, as we cross the boundaries that we have made and step more fully into our life's mission, the glory of your name, we pray.
All:	**Amen.**

* * *

Friends, go into this new week
being quick to listen, slow to speak,
and fully prepared to be changed
in both heart and mind.
We will follow in the ways of Christ.
We will seek a more understanding
and compassionate world.
And so now may the love of God,
the grace and generosity of Jesus,
and the abiding friendship of the Spirit
be with us now and evermore.
Amen!

Sunday between September 11 and September 17 inclusive

Proper 19 [24]

LECTIONARY READINGS
Proverbs 1:20–33
Psalm 19
James 3:1–12
Mark 8:27–38

Teach us your names, O God, spoken acts of mercy and justice and grace. May we learn your names, O Jesus, by trusting who you are for us and for all. May we recognize your names, Holy Spirit, in the renewing of our lives and communities. Amen.

* * *

Leader: God of our Saviour Jesus Christ, when we do not follow in your ways,
All: **forgive us, God, and bring us back to you.**
Leader: When we are afraid of what it might cost us if we really opened ourselves to you,
All: **forgive us, God, and bring us back to you.**
Leader: When we allow self-concern to rule all other concerns,
All: **forgive us, God, and bring us back to you.**
Leader: Guide us, O God, and help us follow Jesus and your Holy Wisdom with all our hearts. Amen.

* * *

Wise and wonderful God,
Wisdom is your holy servant.
With cries and whispers
she is speaking to us,
guiding our understanding of your reign.
Together, today, we will listen to Wisdom's voice.
(*Silence*)
Sometimes we do not know how to quiet
the noise and confusion that swirl within us.
Still, we will listen for Wisdom's voice.
(*Silence*)
Many times we have not listened to your Wisdom, O God.
We don't always know how to recognize your voice.
Still, we will listen for Wisdom's voice.
Forgive us for the times we speak before we listen.
Forgive our impatience in listening to you and to others.
Forgive our words that bring anger instead of your
righteousness.
Open our ears and our hearts to hear your servant, Wisdom.
Amen.

Sunday between September 18 and September 24 inclusive

Proper 20 [25]

LECTIONARY READINGS
Proverbs 31:10–31
Psalm 1
James 3:13—4:3, 7–8a
Mark 9:30–37

Loving God, hold us close when we fear or do not understand the way before us. Open us to the ones who await your welcome through us. May our own frailty make us more gracious – and may we rejoice that in caring for others, we welcome you. Amen.

* * *

We come to this place, O God,
at your invitation.
You welcome us all,
and challenge us to welcome one another
in Christ's name.
Help us to recognize
in each person here
the wonderful greatness
that you perccive
and to celebrate each one's worth –
for Christ's sake. Amen.

* * *

God of love and goodness,
today we celebrate the many ways
in which your Spirit encourages
and leads your people
along the challenging path of Jesus.

Christ, be our strength
and fill us with your wisdom and care.
For those who teach,
those who heal,
those who parent,
and for those who listen intently;
for those who advocate,
those who create art and beauty of any kind
and for those who offer themselves
without even trying.
Christ, be our strength
and fill us with your wisdom and care.
For those who provide aid,
those who rebuild shattered communities
and for those who dream of better worlds,
speaking it into being.
For those who legislate,
keep the peace, put out fires,
or simply offer a welcoming smile.
Christ, be our strength
and fill us with your wisdom and care.
For the world, we pray, O God.
For its healing
and growing up into the ways of love,
we hope and yearn.
And so, in small and significant ways,
continue to use us.
Continue to stand in the midst of us.
Be our strength
and fill us with your wisdom and care.

* * *

Child:	Here we are again, God.
Youth:	Yes, back where we belong
Adult:	At home in the circle of love.
All:	**At home in the circle of love.**
Child:	Greet us in the centre.
Youth:	Yes, hold us in your heart;
Adult:	for we are at peace in the circle of love.
All:	**At peace in the circle of love. Amen.**

* * *

Very often, O God,
we think all that makes sense,
and all that should really concern us,
is our present and future reality;
our needs and *our* ambitions.
And despite all good intention –
years of church going,
community service, searching prayer –
we return to you confessing,
even lamenting out inability
to see past our own noses when it really counts.
When self-centredness rises
like a destructive wave,
or when the need to be great or first in line
blinds us to another
and pushes them to the outer limits
of our care and conscience (*pause*).
Forgive us again, O Holy One.
Centred in your welcome, playful in your arms,
may we find a renewed capacity
and the hard-fought freedom
to be a people of warmth, a people of equality,
indeed, a people of sheer goodness and grace.
Amen.

* * *

Leader: May you be like trees
 planted by streams of water,
 yielding fruit,
 and providing share
 in all the seasons of your life.
 May you prosper in everything
 under the watchful care of God.
 Go forth in joy to love and serve God.
All: **Thanks to be God!**

Sunday between September 25 and October 1 inclusive

Proper 21 [26]

LECTIONARY READINGS
Esther 7:1–6, 9–10, 9:20–22
Psalm 124
James 5:13–20
Mark 9:38–50

Strengthen us, O God, to choose to live faithfully in all the situations we face. Make us bold and courageous advocates for those who are facing danger or risk. Help us be wise, persistent stewards of all that you entrust into our care. Amen.

* * *

Wisdom dances in creation
bringing to life a spirit-filled world.
Wisdom's ways are right and true
and blessed are we who follow.
Come, let us seek the ways of wisdom.

Wisdom's voice is heard
in the deep simplicity of a child's insight,
in the stir of youthful challenge,
and in the certainties and questions of adult faith.
Come, let us seek the ways of wisdom.

When wisdom takes root among us
justice is found through peaceful means
and all creation is pleased.
Come, let us seek the ways of wisdom
and live in communion with God and creation.

* * *

O Divine Wisdom, Sophia of God,
dance among us this day.
Reveal to us the ways of God
and gift us with courage
so we can face each situation
with confidence in your presence and love.

* * *

Opening Prayer
Invite the community to come forward, take a handful of salt from a bowl and then create a design on tables covered in black paper. The design created by each person will symbolize how they will open themselves to God's presence this day. People can create these designs by either pouring salt on the paper and tracing in salt with their fingers, or by creating lines by holding the salt in a closed fist, while allowing a small amount to pour out of the bottom of the hand, between the little finger and the palm.
Once everyone has had a chance to create a symbol, a worship leader moves beside the table, and says:
Our spirits are open to you, O God. Amen.

* * *

God of all our hopes and longings, you fill us with desire and courage to live life to its fullest. We trust in you and give thanks for your presence in all the stages of our lives. You are the breath of our sighing, the prayer of our longing, the song of our praise. You give our actions meaning and help all things to work together for good – even the difficult things. We thank you for this time that you have given us in which to live our lives. Help us to cherish each moment and each person placed upon our path and in our story. In Jesus' name we pray. Amen.

* * *

One: Holy One.
You awaken love in our midst
calling us into a spirit of grace and generosity.
All: We give thanks for your gift of love.
One: You surround us with diversity
calling us into a spirit of compassion and acceptance.
All: We give thanks for your gift of diversity.
One: You reveal beauty in each day
calling us into a spirit of wonder and gratitude.
All: We give thanks for your gift of beauty.
One: You listen to us with tenderness
calling us into a spirit of prayer and reflection.
(*Prayers of concern are offered.*)
All: We give thanks for your gift of listening.
One: You embrace each one of us as your own
calling us into a spirit of courage and confidence.
All: We give thanks for your gift of embrace.
One: Holy One,
Your gifts to use are many.
Our hearts are full.
Our spirits are grateful.
All: Amen.

Sunday between October 2 and October 8 inclusive

Proper 22 [27]

LECTIONARY READINGS
Job 1:1, 2:1–10
Psalm 26
Hebrews 1:1–4, 2:5–12
Mark 10:2–16

God, sometimes we are confused and troubled. We know you are present in our lives, but sometimes that presence can seem elusive or even troublesome. Remind us that you are here no matter what, and that you love us no matter what. Amen.

* * *

Sacred Presence,
from a world of injustice and pain, brokenness and frailty
we come seeking grace,
longing to be enfolded by love.
We seek to be challenged by Jesus' teachings
and the faithful witness of our ancestors in faith.
We long to be shaped and formed into compassionate community.

* * *

Gracious God, you are the hope of all the earth.
Everywhere we turn, you are there,
loving your creation in the midst of all our struggles.
You have given us hearts that question suffering
and minds that resist easy answers.
Be with us now as we ponder
the mysteries of existence
and the part you have called us to play in your amazing world.
Amen.

* * *

Who are the ones you would have us bring into the circle, O God? Who are the ones you would have us speak for – not because it is polite, but because it is just? May we speak and act for all people as you have spoken and acted for us. Amen.

* * *

Some mothers brought children
to Jesus one day,
to have Jesus hold them,
to bless them and pray.
"No, no," said some people
and pushed them away.
"Don't come bother Jesus.
He's busy today.
"This jumping and running
makes way to much noise.
Now take them away,
both the girls and the boys."
But Jesus said, "Come
children *do* jump and run.
Bring all children to me
I'll bless every one."

* * *

Don't be afraid.
Life is so complex and uncertain, O God.
Moments of togetherness
can quickly turn into feelings
of loss, fear, or estrangement.
In the short space of one day,
all can be turned on its head
and we are left longing for familiarity,
crying out for wholeness and hope.
Don't be afraid.
We confess in such seasons of life
our grief, hurt, and anxiety
can unnecessarily distance us
from you and others;
a keen sense of brokenness
becoming but a barrier to needed healing,
and a poor excuse
for prolonged anger and bitterness.
Don't be afraid.
And so we turn again to you
seeking an embrace of love and mercy
to help ease the pain –
to give courage and grace for the living.
Secure in your enfolding arms,
may we dare to trust and let go.
Re-finding our rest and hope
for the journey onwards.

Sunday between October 9 and October 15 inclusive

Proper 23 [28] Thanksgiving Sunday

LECTIONARY READINGS
Job 23:1–9, 16–17
Psalm 22:1–15
Hebrews 4:12–16
Mark 10:17–31

We celebrate your love and presence, O God. May we trust that love and respond to your presence when your call cuts against our expectations or plans. Open us, then, to your compassion that seeks not what is easy for us, but what is best. Amen.

* * *

Look at me with
eyes of love,
Lord Jesus. And
in seeing me for
who I am, help
me to understand
who I may yet
be, according to
your grace. As you
see, may I follow
– with my love,
with my all. Amen.

* * *

One: When God seems distant,
All: we seek what we long to find.
Two: When life overtakes us,
All: we seek what we long to find.
Three: When trouble is near and danger is close,
All: we seek what we long to find.
One: Come find in this place the One we both long to find and who longs to find us.

* * *

Source of Life (*arms reaching up*),
gather us into your presence and hold us in love
    (*draw arms across chest into a hug*).
Make us mindful of the bounty that surrounds us
    (*arms wide to the side*).
Open us to receiving the blessings of this day
    (*hands cupped in front*).
So that we might give generously and freely
    (*palms facing out spread arms to the side*),
in the way that we have been so richly blessed to receive
    (*arms brought across chest*).
Amen.

* * *

Invite the people to stretch their arms out to the side, moving away from each other until everyone is at least an arm's length away from the next person. Advise them that some may have to spill into the aisles or another seating area in order to achieve the distance. Do not begin the prayer of confession until everyone has found a place to stand. Before you begin the prayer, invite them to lower their arms.

Leader: Everlasting God,
we have created distance between us.
These few steps
remind us of the distance that is often between us
and others,
a distance created by careless words and actions,
a deliberate pulling back from commitments,
and the wilful wounding of creation.
We confess that, as it is with our neighbour,
so it is with you, O God.
There is distance between us, too.
Only your grace can bridge that gap,
and every gap that sin creates.
We ask Jesus Christ to take our hand
and walk with us across that bridge,
and leave the distance behind us.
Let us be together with you,
as your people,
for we pray by the power of the Holy Spirit.
All: **Amen.**

* * *

Self-giving God,
for those who remain voiceless
and hungry in our world,
for those targeted by greed
and crass opportunism:
Hear our prayer for the serving with Jesus.
For those who remain attached
to their privilege and wealth,
unable to see their neighbour's need
due to a materialism that blinds and binds:
Hear our prayer for the changing with Jesus.
Hear our prayer, O Holy One.
Take us down new paths of giving
and human possibility.
In the name of Jesus Christ. Amen.

* * *

Words of assurance
In the same way that Jesus
looked upon the rich young ruler
with eyes of compassion,
so too does God view us.
For only love can set us free
to truly give of what we have
and who we are.
Thanks be to God. Amen!

* * *

One: Beloved friends,
God's love is more profound than any of our resistance.
God's forgiveness goes deeper than our despair.
God is with us in all times and places.
Receive God's love.
Receive God's forgiveness
and be healed.
All: Thanks be to God. Amen.

* * *

Sunday between October 16 and October 22 inclusive

Proper 24 [29]

LECTIONARY READINGS
Job 38:1–7, (34–41)
Psalm 104:1–9, 24, 35
Hebrews 5:1–10
Mark 10:35–45

Patient God, we have so many questions. We demand things, and often want to know where the path will lead before we set out. Set our hearts to rest and remind us that life is made up of more questions than answers, and that's okay. Amen.

* * *

O Great Spirit, we gather in your greatness reflected in all creation. With humble hearts we open ourselves to the wisdom of your word, the tenderness of your compassion, and the challenge of your gospel. Redirect our living with your cup of self-giving and your baptism of service. Amen.

* * *

The writer of Hebrews 5 suggests that great spiritual leaders acknowledge their own weaknesses. In the silence of this moment, you are invited to bring to mind your own wounds and weaknesses, shortcomings, and regrets and to hold them before God in silent prayer. (*If you have a prayer bell, ring it to mark the beginning and end of this silence*).

* * *

One: The one who knows weakness deals patiently with the failings of others.
All: **So it is with us when we acknowledge our own failings.**
One: Let us live as people honoured by God despite our shortcomings, called to serve others with gentleness and grace.

* * *

Leader: Our minds are filled with questions.
In faith we call out to be heard.
All: **We long to be near you, O God.**
Leader: Our bodies and souls are weary.
In faith we call out for your healing touch.
All: **We long to be near you, O God.**
Leader: Our hearts wrestle with doubt and wonder about the world around us.
In faith we call out for a foundation that cannot be shaken.
All: **We long to be near you, O God.**
Leader: O, God, how great are the works of your hand!
In wisdom you have made them all.
In faith, we come near to you in worship.
Bless us with the power of your Spirit
and hear our call to you.

Sunday between October 23 and October 29 inclusive

Proper 25 [30]

LECTIONARY READINGS
Job 42:1–6, 10–17
Psalm 34:1–8, (19–22)
Hebrews 7:23–28
Mark 10:46–52

God, when others cry out, help us to listen and not turn them away. When their cries are to us, give us the strength and courage to respond on your behalf. When we cry out to you, help us to listen then, too, and rejoice in the answers you give. Amen.

* * *

We bless you, Holy One, for we know we may cry out to you. We cry out to you, Christ among us, for we trust you to hear. We trust in you, Blessed Spirit, for providing the power to do good, the grace to heal, and the call to follow on the way. Amen.

* * *

Source of goodness, we long to see your face and hear you call our name. We covet your grace and are eager to follow the way of Jesus. Meet us in our deepest needs and call us forth to journey with you and one another. Amen.

* * *

Come, friends.
Come and experience God's goodness
with all your being.
Taste, and touch,
see, and hear,
smell, and wonder,

know, and believe.
Know that in this place
God will hear the cries of
every voice and every heart.
Come, and let us proclaim together
the goodness of our God.

* * *

Invite people to suggest names of persons who have been influential in the shaping and developing of your church. Include famous names of the past, from your own or other denominations and traditions, as well as those who have been significant in the life of your local congregation. Consider theologians, artists, musicians, poets, teachers, and those who have spoken with prophetic voices.

God of new beginnings,
this day we remember and celebrate
those who challenge us
to see things in new ways,
to expand and explore our sense
of what it means to be the Body of Jesus Christ.
We give you thanks for the many people
(*insert here the names of people significant in your tradition,
community, and congregation*)
whose words,
images, music, sermons, writings, questions, ideas,
and laughter
have helped to shape us as a church.
God of our past, our present, and our future,
thank you for those who have gone before us
and who share the wisdom of the ages with us all.
We thank you for those who are young
or new to our community,
who bring a freshness and new way of understanding,

whose new questions invite us, to reflect on the past
and plan for the future.
Pour out your Holy Spirit on us.
Give us courage to let our future
be guided by the Spirit's wind.
We put our trust in you, O God,
trusting that, through all the changes,
the seasons, and the re-formations of our lives,
you are ever with us. Amen.

* * *

Invite the community to consider silently the question: What am I crying out for, and how might others, or I, stop this cry from being heard?

Many voices shout out…
BE QUIET!
To the one who is homeless and says to Jesus.
"I want a place to call my own;
a table for my bread and meat,
a warm blanket to sleep under
and some work to sustain my daily living" (*pause*).

Many voices shout out…
BE QUIET!
To the youth who is delinquent and says to Jesus,
"I want some peace of mind;
an end to the angry voices
that drive me to paths of self destruction.
I need someone to say I am worth something
in this mess of a world" (*pause*).

Many voices shout out…
BE QUIET!
To the one who is gay and says to Jesus,

"I want to come out of this closet,
long shut by misunderstanding and fear;
I want to honestly love someone
in a way that is life-giving and free" (*pause*).

Many voices shout out…
BE QUIET!
Yet Jesus says, "Come here."

Many voices shout out…
BE QUIET!
And the silent spring up and run.

Many voices shout out…
BE QUIET!
And Jesus asks, "What can I do for you?"

Many voices shout out…
BE QUIET!
Yet the grace of Christ rises above the clamour
and fearlessly strides on before us.

* * *

As the cherished of God we have gathered
and as the renewed of God we now depart.
Friends, cry out to be heard,
giving voice to yours and others' needs.
In all you say and do,
seek always the kindness of Christ
and follow with your whole heart.
Be filled with Spirit
and be led into the daily challenges
of life by Spirit's rare and enduring beauty.
Go in peace, and live into wholeness,
now and always.

Sunday between October 30 and November 5 inclusive

Proper 26 [31]

LECTIONARY READINGS
Ruth 1:1–18
Psalm 146
Hebrews 9:11–14
Mark 12:28–34

With all that you are, O God, may I love you and, through you, all creation. Amen.

* * *

Fill five baskets with small squares of coloured paper; each basket is full of a different colour: red, orange, yellow, green, blue. Set a large basket on the worship table.

One: We come to learn, to see, to live,
to breathe, to dance, to grasp, to give,
love, love, love.
(*Pause.*)
We come to worship.
All: **Let us prepare our hearts for worship.**
One: Is there anger in your hearts?
All: **We lay down our anger before God and one another.**
(*The leader sprinkles the red squares into the large basket.*)
One: Are there worries in your hearts?
All: **We lay down our worries before God and one another.**
(*The leader sprinkles the orange squares into the large basket.*)
One: Is there regret in your hearts?
All: **We lay down our regrets before God and one another.**
(*The leader sprinkles the yellow squares into the large basket.*)
One: Is there envy in your hearts?

All: **We lay down our envy before God and one another.**
(The leader sprinkles the green squares into the large basket.)
One: Is there sadness in your hearts?
All: **We lay down our sadness before God and one another.**
(The leader sprinkles the blue squares into the large basket.)
One: As we create room in our hearts for love, may our lives be wholly transformed.
All: **Spirit, take us as we are into your holy love.**
(The leader gently mixes all colours together.)

* * *

If I'm not for me, who will be? If I'm only for me, what am I? And if not now, when? (Rabbi Hillel, *Pirkei Avot*)

* * *

Leader: God of each unfolding moment, you bring all of creation into being. Again and again we receive your gifts of love and friendship in family and community.
All: **O God, open our hearts to the daily miracles with which we are blessed.**
Leader: We trust that you are with us always and everywhere. Yet we often act as if we do not trust you. We try to keep ourselves safe rather than reaching out to others.
All: **O God, open our hearts to the daily miracles with which we are blessed.**
Leader: Sometimes we do not even care for ourselves, and unable to care for others. We let fear inhibit our courage. We find it difficult to love.
All: **O God, open our hearts to the daily miracles with which we are blessed.**
Leader: Forgive us, O God, and help us to find your life-giving presence in every moment we live and every person we meet. Amen.

* * *

Creator of the mountain and the valley,
keeper of the forest and the desert,
companion along the smooth path and the rocky road,
guide toward the light and comfort in the shadows:
We come before you and one another,
with all of our beauty and with all of our needs,
all of our certainties and all of our anxieties,
our deepest regrets and our highest hopes.
We come longing to be changed and transformed
into the image of love. Amen.

* * *

Even in the deep and shadowed places we are not alone.
In the hard times we are nurtured, renewed, and made whole.
God is with us in this journey.
Spirit rejoices with us along the way.
For all the extraordinary and subtle ways that love prevails,
thanks be to God!
Amen.

* * *

You, O Sacred Presence,
are always and everywhere.
We may be blown around
by winds of change and uncertainty,
but you keep faith forever.
You are a steady companion on the way
and we find rest and peace in you.
Amen.

* * *

We thank you, God, for deep and lasting relationships
that give without counting the cost.
We thank you for that great commandment
to love God with all our heart, soul, mind, and strength
and our neighbours as ourselves.

We thank you for women, men, and children
who declare the good news of your love;
for all families, however they were formed,
and for all who seek to love and support others
in their journeying through this life.

* * *

Sacred Presence is always and everywhere
and we know this Presence most fully
in the love of this community,
in the joy of watching children at play,
in the brilliant colours of creation,
and in friends we can turn to in times of need.
Go, confident in the eternal love of God
who is with you wherever you are.
Amen.

Sunday between November 6 and November 12 inclusive

Proper 27 [32]

LECTIONARY READINGS
Ruth 3:1–5, 4:13–17
Psalm 127
Hebrews 9:24–28
Mark 12:38–44

God of truth and grace, I give you thanks for opportunities to give. Teach me not only where my gifts may best be used, but how I might give wholly of myself to you and to others. Amen.

* * *

God of all the small things, may those without voice be championed, those without hope be comforted, those without faith be uplifted. May we be rich in courage as we confront the greed that leads to oppression. May we be rich in compassion as we lament with the brokenhearted. Amen.

* * *

(Inspired by Psalm 127)
Unless it is you, Redeeming One,
who works within and among us,
our efforts are for nothing.
May we find rest in your presence
for our anxious and over-worked lives.
And from the centre of this peace,
may we become mindful of a deep joy and happiness
for the gifts of life around us:
for laughter and friendship,
food that sustains and delights,
hospitality expressed and received,
and for each generation. Amen.

* * *

Leader: Loving God,
we bring to you our prayers of concern.
For this privilege, we also give thanks.
Lord in your mercy,
All: hear our prayer.
Leader: We stand together in your house of worship.
We pray for members of this congregation,
for family and friends,
and we pray for those who have no one to pray for them.
God, in your mercy,
All: hear our prayer.
Leader: We stand together in your house of worship
to pray for your creation,
to bring the work for conservation, preservation,
and reclamation
for your support and blessing.
We pray for all those who help us
to make ethical choices in caring for our environment.
God, in your mercy,
All: hear our prayer.
Leader: We stand together in your house of worship.
to pray for people living in fear,
to bring the victims of war and oppression,
and the targets of persecution and hate,
for your protection and advocacy.
We pray for deliverance from that
which divides the world you love.
Bring us to each other in peace.
God, in your mercy,
All: hear our prayer.
Leader: We stand together in your house of worship.
Unless God builds the house,
those who build labour in vain.
Build this house to the glory of God.
God, in your mercy,
All: hear our prayers.

* * *

When we choose to worry, we lose sight of hope.
When we choose to grumble, we lose sight of joy.
When we choose to fear, we lose sight of love.
When we are worried and grumbling and afraid,
we lose our sight.
God of every vision,
help us to see and to choose what is good. Amen.

* * *

Restored in spirit,
may we take new risks in service.
Renewed in body and mind,
may we join God in creating justice for all.
Secure in new hope,
may we live with joy into the future.
Go in love to give birth to love,
carrying hope into all the world.

Sunday between November 13 and November 19 inclusive

Proper 28 [33]

LECTIONARY READINGS
1 Samuel 1:4–20
1 Samuel 2:1–10
Hebrews 10:11–14, (15–18), 19–25
Mark 13:1–8

God of our life, impatiently we stamp our feet, yelling "now!" Yet empty, we are filled with your life; desperate, we are gifted with your hope; unable to see your future, you open our eyes to faith. May it be in the waiting that we find you. Amen.

* * *

Eternal God, help us to discern and hold fast to your presence in the midst of every changing circumstance, that we may live with hope and love with courage at all times. Amen.

* * *

Have a group perform the following motions.
Spirit of Life
(*extend right arm out to the side*),
come unto me
(*extend left arm out to the side*).
Sing in my heart
(*bring both hands over heart*)
all the stirrings of compassion
(*turn cupped hands away from heart, palms up*).
Blow in the wind
(*draw both arms in an arch over head, left to right*),
rise in the sea
(*touch toes and lift arms over head*),

move in the land
(*clasp hands together over head*),
giving life the shape of justice
(*bring clasped hands down in front of heart*).
Roots hold me close
(*touch toes and lift arms over head*),
wings set me free
(*draw both arms in an arch over head, left to right*),
Spirit of Life
(*extend right arm out to side*),
come unto me
(*extend left arm out to the side*),
come to me
(*lift arms up slightly*).

* * *

Ask the question: What is your deepest longing in this moment? Provide several minutes of silent reflection time. You may choose to play instrumental music that does not demand attention, but adds to the reflection. Conclude with the spoken prayer.
When our deepest longings crash against us like waves
and threaten to pull us into a sea of hopelessness,
we pour out our souls to you (*pause*).
When our happiness seems like distant stars –
unattainable, dim, and clouded from view,
we pour out our souls to you (*pause*).
When our future is uncertain,
like a cloudy night sky,
we pour out our souls to you (*pause*).

* * *

Have a child offer these words to the congregation.
Our prayers are heard
by one who is always good.
God knows the desires of our hearts
and fills us with love.
Peace be with you.

* * *

Hearer of our words, but especially our hearts,
welift our prayers to you,
as we ask that you fill every emptiness
of our souls with your hope, your love, your grace,
O God, we call.
For those who live with no future
or no hope,
for those who are belittled by others,
O God, we call.
Give us the words to speak on behalf of the mothers in developing
countries and inner cities,
cradling their hungry children in their arms.
Enable us to remember, with you,
those held captive by war and violence,
pain and addiction, brokenness and despair.
O God, we call.
Make us mindful of the lonely, the friendless, the forgotten.
Intensify our compassion,
deepen our concern,
enlarge our hearts with your grace.
O God, we call.

* * *

All:	**We go to create a world of justice and joy.**
One:	For everyone born…
Two:	fresh water to drink.
One:	For everyone born…
Two:	someone to love them.
One:	For everyone born…
Two:	enough food to eat.
One:	For everyone born…
Two:	friendship and laughter.
One:	For everyone born…
Two:	a space where they're safe.
One:	For everyone born…
Two:	somewhere to sleep.
One:	For everyone born…
Two:	a life filled with hope
All:	**We go to create a world of justice and joy. Amen.**

* * *

Giver of wonder,
when we think our resources are scarce, you bless us,
so that others might be filled,
so that prayers might be answered,
so that hope might be shared,
so your reign might come for all. Amen.

Reign of Christ or Christ the King Sunday

Proper 29 [34]

LECTIONARY READINGS
2 Samuel 23:1–7
Psalm 132:1–12, (13–18)
Revelation 1:4b–8
John 18:33–37

Alpha and Omega, you encircle time with your presence, you encircle creation with your love. You brought all things into being and receive all things back to you. May we find our hope, and our life, in your enfolding grace. Amen.

* * *

God of our lives, in your truth, the marginalized are role models, the voiceless sing words of hope the world needs to hear, the powerless gain strength from your faithful witness. Reign over us, tender God, so we may dwell in the beauty of your realm. Amen.

* * *

Like leaves skipping over the carpet of grass:
God comes to us, the One who was and is and is to come.
Like the first glimpses of the sun peeking over the horizon:
God comes to us, the One who was and is and is to come.
Like the moon lighting our way on a cloudless, autumn night:
God comes to us, the One who was and is and is to come.
We have chosen to be here, where God remembers us.
God comes to us, the One who was and is and is to come.

* * *

Almighty God,
from the beginning of time
to the end of eternity,
you have chosen
to use your power and majesty
to love us,
to redeem us,
to shape us as your people.
Your reign is in our midst, God of all people.
Spirit of God,
resting upon us:
may your power enflame us
with your peace;
may your peace touch us
with your grace;
may your grace fill us
with your hope;
may your hope lead us
always in your path.
Spirit of gentleness, you are in our very midst. Amen.

✷ ✷ ✷

God of ends and beginnings,
of timeless circles of forever,
we celebrate this day
the Reign of Christ:
child of David, and of Mary,
sovereign of eternity,
servant leader, witness of truth,
and governor of our lives.
Help us renew our commitment and covenant
to be disciples and leaders.
Help us live with the example and ministry of this same Christ
in whose name we both worship and pray. Amen.

✷ ✷ ✷

Friends, grace to you and peace
from the One who is
and who was
and who is to come.
And also to you!
We gather in the love of Christ
to be centered and stilled.
We open our hearts to receive anew.
We open our hearts to the mercy of Christ,
who is our healing and wholeness.
We open our minds to receive anew.
We open our ears to the wisdom of Christ,
who is our grounding and inspiration.
We open our lives to receive anew.

✷ ✷ ✷

After receiving the offering, invite people to form a circular shape that works in your worship space, moving around and through the seating area as needed. Remain in this circle through the sending forth.

Leader: Into this circle of your hope and promise
    we place our lives,
    O God of all times and places.
    In the circle of hope
    we make our offering to you.
    Receive these gifts and use them
    by the power of your Spirit
    to widen the circle of your reign
    through ministry in the name of Jesus Christ.
All: Amen.

HEBREW SCRIPTURES INDEX

Genesis 1:1–5 25
Genesis 9:8–17 47
Genesis 17:1–7, 15–16 51

Exodus 20:1–17 54

Numbers 21:4–9 56

Deuteronomy 18:15–20 33

Ruth 1:1–18 169
Ruth 3:1–5, 4:13–17 173

1 Samuel 1:4–20 176
1 Samuel 2:1–10 176
1 Samuel 3:1–10, (11–20) 27
1 Samuel 8:4–11, (12–15),
    16–20, (11:14–15) 95
1 Samuel 15:34—16:13 98
1 Samuel 17:(1a, 4–11, 19–23),
    32–49 102

2 Samuel 1:1, 17–27 108
2 Samuel 5:1–5, 9–10 112
2 Samuel 6:1–5, 12b–19 115
2 Samuel 7:1–11, 16 13
2 Samuel 7:1–14a 119
2 Samuel 11:1–15 122

2 Samuel 11:26—12:13a 125
2 Samuel 18:5–9, 15, 31–33 129
2 Samuel 23:1–7 180

1 Kings 2:10–12, 3:3–14 133
1 Kings 8:(1, 6, 10–11),
    22–30, 41–43 137

2 Kings 2:1–12 44
2 Kings 5:1–14 37

Esther 7:1–6, 9–10, 9:20–22 ... 153

Job 1:1, 2:1–10 156
Job 23:1–9, 16–17 159
Job 38:1–7, (34–41) 163
Job 42:1–6, 10–17 165

Psalm 1 .... 85, 149
Psalm 4 74
Psalm 9:9–20 102
Psalm 14 122
Psalm 19 .... 54, 147
Psalm 20 98
Psalm 22:1–15 159
Psalm 22:23–31 51
Psalm 22:25–31 80
Psalm 23 76

Psalm 24 115	Psalm 133 71
Psalm 25:1–10 47	Psalm 138 95
Psalm 26 156	Psalm 139:1–6, 13–18 27
Psalm 29 .... 25, 91	Psalm 146 169
Psalm 30 37	Psalm 147:1–11, 20c 35
Psalm 31:9–16 63	Psalm 148 21
Psalm 34:1–8, (19–22) 165	
Psalm 41 41	Proverbs 1:20–33 147
Psalm 45:1–2, 6–9 139	Proverbs 22:1–2, 8–9, 22–23 .. 143
Psalm 48 112	Proverbs 31:10–31 149
Psalm 50:1–6 44	
Psalm 51:1–12 .... 59, 125	Song of Solomon 2:8–13 139
Psalm 62:5–12 30	
Psalm 72:1–7, 10–14 23	Isaiah 6:1–8 91
Psalm 80:1–7, 17–19 7	Isaiah 25:6–9 67
Psalm 84 137	Isaiah 40:1–11 9
Psalm 85:1–2, 8–13 9	Isaiah 40:21–31 35
Psalm 89:1–4, 19–26 13	Isaiah 43:18–25 41
Psalm 89:20–37 119	Isaiah 50:4–9a 63
Psalm 98 .... 17, 83	Isaiah 52:7–10 17
Psalm 104:1–9, 24, 35 163	Isaiah 60:1–6 23
Psalm 104:24–34, 35b 87	Isaiah 61:1–4, 8–11 11
Psalm 107:1–3, 17–22 56	Isaiah 61:10—62:3 21
Psalm 111 .... 33, 133	Isaiah 64:1–9 7
Psalm 118:1–2, 14–24 67	
Psalm 118:1–2, 19–29 63	Jeremiah 31:31–34 59
Psalm 119:9–16 59	
Psalm 124 153	Ezekiel 37:1–14 87
Psalm 125 143	
Psalm 126 11	Jonah 3:1–5, 10 30
Psalm 127 173	
Psalm 130 .... 108, 129	
Psalm 132:1–12, (13–18) 180	

NEW TESTAMENT INDEX

Matthew 2:1–12 23

Mark 1:1–8 9
Mark 1:4–11 25
Mark 1:9–15 47
Mark 1:14–20 30
Mark 1:21–28 33
Mark 1:29–39 35
Mark 1:40–45 37
Mark 2:1–12 41
Mark 3:20–35 95
Mark 4:26–34 98
Mark 4:35–41 102
Mark 5:21–43 108
Mark 6:1–13 112
Mark 6:14–29 115
Mark 6:30–34, 53–56................ 119
Mark 7:1–8, 14–15, 21–23 139
Mark 7:24–37 143
Mark 8:27–38 147
Mark 8:31–38 51
Mark 9:2–9 .... 44, 51
Mark 9:30–37 149
Mark 9:38–50 153
Mark 10:2–16 156
Mark 10:17–31 159
Mark 10:35–45 163
Mark 10:46–52 165

Mark 11:1–11 63
Mark 12:28–34 169
Mark 12:38–44 173
Mark 13:1–8 176
Mark 13:24–37 7
Mark 14:1—15:47 63
Mark 15:1–39, (40–47).............. 63
Mark 16:1–8 67

Luke 1:26–38 13
Luke 1:47–55 .... 11, 13
Luke 2:22–40 21
Luke 24:36b–48.......................... 74

John 1:1–14................................. 17
John 1:6–8, 19–28...................... 11
John 1:43–51 27
John 2:13–22 54
John 3:1–17................................. 91
John 3:14–21 56
John 6:1–21.............................. 122
John 6:24–35 125
John 6:35, 41–51 129
John 6:51–58 133
John 6:56–69 137
John 10:11–18 76
John 12:12–16 63
John 12:20–33 59

John 15:1–8 80	2 Corinthians 4:13—5:1 95
John 15:9–17 83	2 Corinthians 5:6–10,
John 15:26–27, 16:4b–15 87	(11–13), 14–17 98
John 17:6–19 85	2 Corinthians 6:1–13 102
John 18:33–37 180	2 Corinthians 8:7–15 108
John 20:1–18 67	2 Corinthians 12:2–10 112
John 20:19–31 71	
	Galatians 4:4–7 21
Acts 1:15–17, 21–26 85	
Acts 2:1–21 87	Ephesians 1:3–14 115
Acts 3:12–19 74	Ephesians 2:1–10 56
Acts 4:5–12 76	Ephesians 2:11–22 119
Acts 4:32–35 71	Ephesians 3:1–12 23
Acts 8:26–40 80	Ephesians 3:14–21 122
Acts 10:34–43 67	Ephesians 4:1–16 125
Acts 10:44–48 83	Ephesians 4:25—5:2 129
Acts 19:1–7 25	Ephesians 5:15–20 133
	Ephesians 6:10–20 137
Romans 4:13–25 51	
Romans 8:12–17 91	Philippians 2:5–11 63
Romans 8:22–27 87	
Romans 16:25–27 13	1 Thessalonians 5:16–24 11
1 Corinthians 1:3–9 7	Hebrews 1:1–4, (5–12) 17
1 Corinthians 1:18–25 54	Hebrews 1:1–4, 2:5–12 156
1 Corinthians 6:12–20 27	Hebrews 4:12–16 159
1 Corinthians 7:29–31 30	Hebrews 5:1–10 163
1 Corinthians 8:1–13 33	Hebrews 5:5–10 59
1 Corinthians 9:16–23 35	Hebrews 7:23–28 165
1 Corinthians 9:24–27 37	Hebrews 9:11–14 169
	Hebrews 9:24–28 173
2 Corinthians 1:18–22 41	Hebrews 10:11–14, (15–18),
2 Corinthians 4:3–6 44	19–25 176

Index

James 1:17–27 139
James 2:1–10, (11–13),
    14–17 143
James 3:1–12 147
James 3:13—4:3, 7–8a 149
James 5:13–20 153

1 Peter 3:18–22 47

2 Peter 3:8–15a 9

1 John 1:1—2:2 71
1 John 3:1–7 74
1 John 3:16–24 76
1 John 4:7–21 80
1 John 5:1–6 83
1 John 5:9–13 85

Revelation 1:4b–8 180